A Reader's Guide to
Religious Literature

A Reader's Guide to Religious Literature

BEATRICE BATSON

MOODY PRESS • Chicago

FIRST PRINTING

Library of Congress Catalog Card Number: 68-18889

Contents

CHAPTER   PAGE

Preface 7

1. The Middle Ages and the Renaissance 9

2. The Seventeenth Century 32

3. The Eighteenth Century 95

4. The Nineteenth Century 124

5. The Twentieth Century 155

  Footnotes 177

  For Further Reading 180

  Index 184

Preface

IT IS OFTEN STATED that the primary purpose of the imaginative writer is not to convert but to reveal. And rather than working within the confines of a particular sector of political, moral or religious beliefs, he can escape all categories of limitation by exploring the deeper dimensions of man. One can, I believe, accept this statement and still use the term "religious" literature. This does not imply that the author is seeking to propagandize his beliefs, but rather to reveal through his writings a vision of life springing from his religious perspective. Thinking readers are aware that a piece of writing does not achieve the status of literature just because it concerns lofty subjects like God or immortality or heaven. On the other hand, one does not fail to write authentic literature if he grapples with or reflects upon such subjects from a God-oriented position. What actually makes a work live as literature is a vividness and depth of perception in presenting honestly and artistically the conflicts, dilemmas and experiences of life.

This handbook is not designed to minimize *any* great literature, but to examine the writings of honest, creative authors whose vision of life reveals their God-oriented position. And the primary basis for the selection of these works is their God-oriented thrust or perspective, not simply their Christian themes. The qualities which have been suggested as characterizing literature worthy of the name have also served as standards for judgment.

Writers from the early Middle Ages to the twentieth century are included. Great works such as Augustine's *Confessions,* Dante's *Divine Comedy* and Milton's *Paradise Lost* receive a more thorough examination than do works of less literary renown.

Each chapter contains a brief survey of the most significant historical and cultural developments of the period discussed. Numerous references are made to works of literature which are characteristic of the period, even though they may not be considered religious literature. Each literary work singled out for special study is described in detail and a concise biography of its writer is given. Some selected works of a given author are only briefly discussed. Near the end of each chapter, except the final one, are short descriptions of authors whose contributions cannot be ignored, but whose writings are of less than outstanding literary stature.

The treatment of twentieth century literature is not extensive. It is difficult to predict which writers posterity will call the outstanding religious authors of this century, but a few whose writings seem to contain the seeds of permanency are presented in some depth.

This handbook does not enter into scholarly and critical controversy. It is designed primarily to describe literary works with the hope that the reader will be induced to study carefully the literature itself on his own. Nothing said in this volume can be a substitute for the actual reading of religious literature.

It is regrettable that all literary genres could not be carefully covered, but the scope of the study demanded limitations. Books written primarily for children have not been included; "religious Pollyanna" has been deliberately excluded; and I am sure that some works have been omitted simply because I did not discover them. However, my objective has been to bring together from the various periods *selected* writings that could be labeled religious literature. Except for occasional discussions of a few novels and dramas, poetry and nonfictional prose constitute the major part of *A Reader's Guide to Religious Literature*.

BEATRICE BATSON

CHAPTER 1

The Middle Ages
and the Renaissance

THE PERIOD from the fall of Rome to the Renaissance (c. 500-
1500) is usually referred to as the Middle Ages. Its earliest centuries (c. 500-1000) are still frequently called the Dark Ages.
The period is dark, however, only in comparison with the bril-
liance of the preceding and following eras, and it certainly should
not be regarded as a time of total intellectual decay. After the
age of classical writings, during the rise of the church to pre-
eminence, the orientation of thought shifted decisively to the
otherworldly and the metaphysical. Rigorous intellectual activity
continued, but the focus of interest was not primarily with concerns of this world. The Augustan or Golden Age (30 B.C.-A.D. 14),
which had produced Virgil, Horace, Livy and Ovid, and the Silver
Age (A.D. 14-117), whose literary lights were Seneca, Martial,
Tacitus, Juvenal and Epictetus, gave way to the period of Patristic writings. Produced by the Church Fathers, the Patristic writings were basically defenses of the faith and elaborations on
theological and doctrinal subjects. But these works were not
merely prosaic expositions. Various Church Fathers educated in
the classical tradition were sensitive to the power of literary art in
summing up their thoughts. Origen (c. 185-253), for example,
demonstrated his regard for allegory in his *De Principiis*. Ambrose
(c. 340-397) made abundant uses of symbol and allegory. His
Physiologus is a bestiary which relates religious and moral truths
by allegorical illustrations from the animal kingdom. Jerome (c.
340-420), a remarkable scholar and a contemporary of Ambrose,
made the outstanding contribution of translating the Old Testament into the Latin Vulgate. He also wrote a series of biographies
of prominent Christians.

9

AUGUSTINE (345-430)

Rising above those earlier writers was Aurelius Augustinus who, after years of searching and questioning, became one of the most energetic and intelligent leaders in Western Christendom. Of Roman-African stock, Augustine was born in northern Africa of a pagan father and a Christian mother. He received an excellent education first in the classics and then in law. After a long and circuitous route he brought his talents as a scholar and writer to the service of Christianity. Augustine wrote an enormous amount of Christian-oriented literature of five principal kinds: philosophy, polemics, moral treatises, sermons and apologetics. Of particular interest to the student of literature is his *Confessions*.

THE CONFESSIONS (397)

Composed shortly after he became a bishop, Augustine's *Confessions* reveal penetrating insight into the life, religion and philosophies of his day. But perhaps even more important is the frank unveiling of his personal conflicts as a young man whose passionate body and mind both clamored for satisfaction. Augustine used the spiritual autobiography as the literary type to unfold the candid account of his inner struggles.

"In a purely literary sense," says Harold C. Gardiner, "the *Confessions* are unique. They are actually the first example of true Christian introspection." Although Marcus Aurelius preceded Augustine in recording the probings of his soul, Gardiner says, "He was simply the 'good pagan' communing with a soul which was, however noble, largely empty." Sharpening his perspective, Gardiner then argues: "Augustine was the first to search his soul as God knew it and as Christ redeemed it, and to record those glories in words that are certainly among the most moving and searching of the world's great literature. . . . He is truly a literary pioneer."[1]

At the same time, what brings Augustine closest to the reader and imparts to his *Confessions* a living and enduring interest is that as one reads the narrative of another man's pilgrimage, he finds his own story being told. The large questions that perplexed Augustine are the same that vex any thinking individual of any age who is trying to know himself and the One beyond self. How can one find purpose in life? What is sin? What is the solution to the problem of evil? How can one explain the suffering in the

world if a good God is in control of the universe? What is freedom, and is man really free? How can one know that the God he
loves is the supernatural God and not some fantastic image of his
own mind? These questions plagued Augustine in the fourth
century, and the twentieth century finds none more pressing.
Augustine's questions rose from an honest search, and he wanted
them clarified. There is no indication that he wanted simply to
glorify the struggle or to magnify the anguish of self-examination;
he wanted to *know,* and he wanted a solid basis for his belief.
And his work clearly enunciates that as he questioned and examined, rejected and accepted, he finally found the satisfying
Object of his search.

The *Confessions* open upon Augustine in characteristic dialogue
with God: "Great art Thou, O God, and greatly to be praised. . . .
Grant me Lord, to know and understand which is first, to call on
Thee or to praise Thee? and, again, to know Thee or to call on
Thee? . . . For he that knoweth Thee not may call on Thee as other
than Thou art." These questions simply introduced others, climax-
ing in Augustine's query as to how a finite mind can really know
the infinite One. He assumes in the very first book and contends
throughout that there must be some kind of paradoxical inter-
twining of divine grace and human faith before finite man can
know God. And it is a long journey from his boyhood days in
Thagaste to his conversion in Milan in 386.

Book I continues with Augustine's reflections upon his infancy
and boyhood, recalling in particular some of his childhood pranks
and his rebellious and recalcitrant spirit toward his studies. Surely
some of the pedagogical insights of the "teacher of Carthage"
break through when Augustine, alluding to his early years, says,
"I loved not study, and hated to be forced to it. Yet I was forced;
and this was well done towards me, but I did not well; for unless
forced, I had not learnt. But no one doth well against his will,
even though what he doth be well." Combined with the austerities
of his early education and his utter dislike of the study of Greek,
Augustine speaks of his intense love of Latin and Roman literature. Referring to the latter, Augustine says, "This I learned without any pressure of punishment to urge me on, for my heart urged
me to give birth to its conceptions. . . . No doubt, then, that a free
curiosity has more force in our learning these things than a fright-

ful enforcement." The modernity of this fourth-century thinking is inescapable!

Book II presents more of Augustine as a teen-ager. His sixteenth year, singled out for close concentration, appears to be a critical one in the young man's life. A tightening of family finances forced him to discontinue his studies at the nearby city of Madaura and to spend the year at home, during which he "wallowed" in licentiousness, having joined a medieval gang of "lewd young fellows" whose sins he sought to emulate. One specific deed, stealing pears and wasting them, is lifted out for analysis by Augustine. Why does the writer attach more significance to the pilfering of pears than to "wallowing" in licentiousness? The theft seems to point clearly to the aimlessness and the purposelessness of the young man's life, for he did not really want the pears.

Meanwhile Augustine gave sufficient promise as a student for his father to send him to Carthage to continue his studies. During this period, as he reveals in Book III, stage plays and literature became his chief loves. He also discovered Cicero's *Hortensious* which literally ignited a love for learning and caused him to long "with an incredible burning desire for the immortality of wisdom." He resolved to "bend" his mind to the Holy Scriptures and acknowledged that "with God is wisdom." But he "disdained to be a little one; and swollen with pride," he considered himself "a great one." Nevertheless, fired with a new love for the contemplative life, Augustine began to wrestle with some large human problems, particularly the problem of evil. The Manicheans, whose popular philosophy emphasized a dualism of spirit and matter, not only stimulated his interest in the knotty problem but also captured his admiration by explaining that evil was rooted in matter. Believing, too, that the Manichean principle of two opposing forces of good and evil seemed to correspond with the reality of his own nature, Augustine became more and more interested in Manicheanism, and later aligned himself with this viewpoint for nine years.

Greatly distressed because of Augustine's acceptance of Manicheanism, Monica, his Christian mother, requested a bishop to talk with her son and seek to lead him from such heresy. The bishop considered it unwise to confront Augustine at the time with refutations of Manicheanism, but assured Monica that someday he would discern for himself the erroneous nature of the religion.

Book IV tells of Augustine's completion of his student days at Carthage and of his return to his hometown, Thagaste, where he began teaching literature and rhetoric. During this time he took a mistress or concubine who remained with him until shortly before his conversion to Christianity. Of his relation to this unnamed woman Augustine says: "In those years I had one,—not in that which is called lawful marriage, but whom I had found out in a wayward passion, void of understanding; yet but one, remaining faithful even to her. . . ."

Information on Augustine's return to Carthage, insights on grief, reflections on real and unreal friendship, and the account of the writing of his first book, *Concerning the Beautiful and the Apt*, are also disclosed in Book IV.

Augustine records in Book V that a Manichean leader, Bishop Faustus, visited Carthage. In conversation with the bishop, Augustine discovered that he was ignorant of his professed "superior knowledge." When Augustine questioned the bishop on matters of Manichean doctrine, he either completely evaded them or tried to clothe his vague, ignorant responses in colorful, meaningless words. Augustine's inquisitive, analytical mind could not accept such an undiscerning, faulty, illogical basis for faith. Augustine could appreciate only two aspects of the bishop's pseudoknowledge: "He was not altogether ignorant of his own ignorance, nor would he rashly be entangled in a dispute, whence he could neither retreat nor extricate himself fairly." The encounter with Bishop Faustus convinced Augustine that he was not interested in pursuing the Manichean religion further.

Disillusioned with Manicheanism and further disgusted with the licentious students at Carthage, Augustine traveled to Rome. From Rome he made his way to another teaching position in Milan.

Books VI and VII tell of the arrival of his mother, Monica, in Milan and of her great joy in Augustine's loss of interest in Manicheanism. His mother unceasingly prayed for his conversion, but she wanted to be sure that when he became a Christian he would forsake practices which, though customs of the day, were to her sinful. Consequently, she urged him to dismiss his concubine. Augustine, telling of his sorrow at having to part with her, said

she was "torn from him." He confessed that not long after he
took another concubine.

Motivated by his own desire to "search the more diligently and
despair not," encouraged by the stimulating influence of friends,
and stirred by the life and preaching of Ambrose, Augustine pondered seriously the claims of the Christian faith. He began to
realize that the cause of sin lies in the free will and hence he
could no longer accept Manichean explanations for man's behavior. But the problem of evil still vexed him. Reading widely
in the literature of the Neoplatonists, Augustine continued his
search for a solution to his dilemma. Convinced from his reading
in Neoplatonic thought of the ultimate reality of the Divine Idea,
of which the physical world is an imperfect copy, Augustine conceived of God as spiritual in nature in contrast to the idea of a
God with a material body. This brought partial satisfaction, but
still the concept of the incarnation perplexed him. How could
God come to an evil world and not be soiled by it? But as he
probed the Scriptures and considered the role of Christ as Mediator between divine or ultimate reality and corporeal imperfec-
tion, his questions regarding the incarnation no longer troubled
him.

In Book VIII Augustine with unusual literary power brings together his spiritual autobiography into the tension of a dramatic
climax. His haunting intellectual perplexities were somewhat resolved; his clamoring body in some measure knew satisfaction; several of his close friends were transformed from unbelief to Christianity; and finally, but perhaps most important, there was the
influence of Ambrose "who embodied for Augustine the dignity
of Christian learning and the majesty of the authority of the
Christian Scriptures." The spiritual and intellectual power of
this unpretentious man Augustine found undeniable and inescapable. Augustine struggled with the torment of indecision. Then
one day in a Milanese garden he heard the words "Take up and
read" coming from a voice in a nearby house. This precipitated
the conflict. Interpreting the words as a command from God,
Augustine opened a Bible to Romans 13:13-14 and read the injunction "not in rioting and drunkenness, not in chambering and
wantonness, not in strife and envying. But put ye on the Lord
Jesus Christ, and make not provision for the flesh, to fulfil the
lusts thereof." Conversion experiences may be explained differ-

ently among people who have had a genuine confrontation with the living God. Augustine simply says, "No further would I read; nor needed I: for instantly at the end of this sentence, by a light as it were of serenity infused into my heart, all the darkness of doubt vanished away."

In order to spend time in the country in contemplation and study in preparation for his baptism in 387, Augustine resigned his professorship of rhetoric.

One other significant incident in Augustine's spiritual autobiography must be noted: the death of his mother, the severance of an exceedingly strong earthly tie. Returning to Africa with his mother, Augustine was with her when she died at Ostia in her fifty-sixth year. In the shadow of Monica's approaching death, Augustine describes their ecstatic conversation regarding life and death and tells of his mother's deep satisfaction in knowing that he had become a Christian believer. Following the death of his devout mother, Augustine, worn by sorrow and grief, took comfort in the memory of her strong Christian character and in the assurance that she was "not altogether dead" but was entering into a new life.

In one sense the spiritual autobiography is concluded at the end of Book IX, but neither the *Confessions* nor the story of Augustine are complete. The restless, open mind of Augustine continued to explore. In Books X–XIII Augustine turned to the investigation of philosophical and theological issues on which he reflected until the end of his life. More specifically, in Book X, he explored the interpretation of God's role in creating a world in which awesome personal experiences with an infinite God may be a reality. The essence of Book X may be expressed in yet another way: "the relation of memory to selfhood, and thence of self to God." It is a reflection on man's way to God, a way which begins in a knowledge of self but passes beyond it through "the fields and spacious halls of memory" and even beyond the mystery of memory to that confrontation between the self and the One beyond self. But the story is only half told. Man must also be willing to begin with a God who created *ex nihilo,* who guides the whole course of creation and who will eventually direct it to its consummation. Until one has looked deeply into the mystery of creation, on which all history and individual experience hang, the journey of that awesome encounter between God and self is only partially made.

Students of literature particularly appreciate the rhetorical power of the *Confessions*. Some of Augustine's most eloquent rhetoric is undoubtedly found in Book X, especially in those magnificent phrases: "And what is this? I asked the earth, and it answered me, 'I am not he, . . .' I replied unto all the things which encompass the door of my flesh, 'Ye have told me of my God, that ye are not He, tell me something of Him.' And they cried out with a loud voice, 'He made us.'"

The three last books, omitted in some editions, are analytical and technical. Elaborating upon the creation story in Book XI, Augustine discovers the subject of time meaningless apart from Genesis 1:1, "In the beginning God created the heaven and the earth." Time partakes of the finite and historical like other aspects of creation; it is a measurement comprehensible by the mind of men. But in the mind of an infinite God there is only an eternal present.

In Books XII and XIII Augustine, further scrutinizing Genesis 1:1, concludes that the word "heaven" means that "spiritual and incorporeal creation" and the word "earth" refers to formless matter from which the corporeal creation was formed. He readily admits that the Holy Scripture is of such depth that varieties of scholarly approaches will yield various interpretations, all of which may contain truth. The final book is a continuation of the exposition of Genesis 1 with special emphasis upon the goodness and power of God as manifested in His creation.

Though the last three books, and certainly to some extent the last four, are somewhat technical, it is obvious that Augustine continues throughout these books "the devotional, confessional style of the earlier books. Also, he continues the deft turn of phrases so characteristic of the *Confessions*."[2] The entire work shows deep psychological insight and sharp introspective analysis as an honest, inquiring individual journeys toward God.

The years following Augustine's *Confessions* until about A.D. 800 were not significant ones for literary productions in Western Europe. The single important exception was Boethius' humanistic work, *The Consolation of Philosophy*. The most significant literary work in England was the Anglo-Saxon epic, *Beowulf*, with pagan and Christian elements placed side by side.[3] Other poems, small in poetic stature, also appear. One authentic fragment can be attributed to Caedmon, frequently called the "father of English song." Bede's *Ecclesiastical History,* Book IV, records Caedmon's attendance at a feast where all were required to improvise and sing. Lacking the gift of song, Caedmon left the feast and, after a vision, received ability to sing by supernatural intervention. This resulted in "Hymn to Caedmon," a little religious poem only nine lines in length, in praise to God the Creator. Several other poems have been attributed to Caedmon. Among these is a paraphrase of portions of the Genesis story which contain a few strong poetic passages.

Cynewulf, who lived during the late eighth century, was the author of several important works. "The Christ," perhaps his most significant religious poem, deals with the nativity, the ascension, and the last judgment. Although some passages contain beautiful imagery, the poem suffers from obscurity and lack of unity.

The years from A.D. 800 to 1300 reveal a literature with a variety of characteristics. There were the poems of the Goliards, the growth of vernacular literature, the songs of the troubadours, the romances of the Arthurian cycle, and finally the celebrated thirteenth century poem, *The Romance of the Rose.* But without doubt the greatest of the religious works of the late medieval period was Dante's *Divine Comedy.*

DANTE ALIGHIERI (1265-1321)

Born in Florence, Italy, Dante was a poet and statesman of a prominent Guelf family. The Guelfs, supporting the Papacy, represented the new commercial and industrial class which gave Florence its wealth and power. The Ghibellines, on the other hand, consisted of the feudal nobility whose power was being displaced by the commercial class; they were opposed to papal domination and looked forward to the control of Italy by the emperor. In the ideologically divided city, Dante played a leading political role. In 1289 he fought with the Guelfs against the Ghibellines and helped his faction achieve victory. His political career was crowned with success in 1300 when he became one of the six priors who governed the city. During the same year the Guelfs split into two parties, the "Whites," or moderates, and the "Blacks," or extreme pro-Papists. Dante's friendships included members of both factions although his opposition to the temporal claims of the Pope placed him primarily on the side of the Whites. As the conflict continued, the Blacks were victorious and the Whites—including Dante—were exiled from Florence. Dante never returned to Florence, and little is known of the remaining years of his life except that they were spent largely with a series of patrons in various courts of Italy. He died in Ravenna.

Dante's earliest literary work is *The New Life,* a commemoration of the author's love for one named Beatrice. His next work, *The Banquet,* though never completed, was intended as a banquet of philosophical knowledge for the layman. Of special significance is Dante's famous "four levels of interpretation" presented in the first chapter of Book II. He explains the four meanings to be derived from a text: literal, allegorical, moral and anagogical. Dante presents a spiritual defense of the vernacular in *On the Vulgar Tongue,* and in *On Monarchy* he expounds his views concerning the separation of the temporal and spiritual spheres of government. He calls for a dual authority of one world empire to rule over temporal affairs and one universal church to govern spiritual matters. It is clear that Dante believed that emperors receive their authority from God and not from the Pope. The emperor was responsible to God to rule over temporal matters; the Pope, also responsible to God, was to rule only over spiritual affairs. Many of Dante's convictions expressed in his earlier writings are reiterated in his monumental religious work, *The Divine Comedy.*

THE DIVINE COMEDY (begun *c.* 1307, completed 1321)

The greatness of *The Divine Comedy* proceeds in part from the fact that Dante poured into this masterpiece so many facets of human concern. It is "an encyclopedia which includes nearly all the phases of the Middle Ages: political, social, cultural, scientific, and religious. . . . It is a glorification of love. . . . It is fiercely human in its intense hatred of evil. . . . Its length includes a multitude of dramatic incidents, scenes of horror and visions of bliss . . . and a succession of wonderfully varied poetic images and colorful phrases."[4] But Dante's chief preoccupation in the elaborate allegory is with man and his relationship to God. As one moves downward through the various circles of the Inferno and upward through the terraces of Purgatorio and further around the spheres of Paradiso, he soon discovers that there is one unifying theme: man's lost condition and his need for restoration.

Dante's picture of the physical order of his three divisions helps define the moral and spiritual significance of *The Divine Comedy*. His cosmology follows the Ptolemaic system as devised by the ancients and as adapted to Christian doctrine by scholastic philosophers. Thus the globe of the earth is the center of the cosmos. Around it revolve nine concentric celestial spheres, while a tenth, the Empyrean—the seat of God—is without motion. In the interior of the earth, or rather of the northern hemisphere, like a funnel narrowing down toward the center of the earth, lies Hell. In its lowest part, at the very center of the earth, is the abode of Satan, who in his fall bored far into the earth, pushing aside huge portions of its interior and driving it upward. That portion of the earth is the great Mount Purgatory which covers the whole southern hemisphere. It is a conically shaped mountain, the abode of those awaiting purgation from sins. Finally, on the summit of Mount Purgatory lies the Garden of Eden, the earthly paradise.

Within the three large realms of this poem, Hell, Purgatory and Heaven, Dante finds souls arranged in groups corresponding to their earthly deeds or dispositions. The *Inferno* opens with Dante lost in a dark, wild woods, symbolic of his journey through life. Midway in his journey he realizes he is lost. Lifting his eyes toward the top of a huge mountain, he sees a light and wants to run toward it. But he cannot thus escape, because he finds his way blocked by three beasts, each representative of a type of sin which prevents man from attaining salvation. A She-Wolf represents the sins of incontinence, or self-indulgence; a Lion represents the sins of violence, or bestial sins; and a Leopard represents fraud, or malicious sins. Dante holds that all the sins common to mankind fall into these three categories and man must recognize how blinding and destructive sin is before he sees ultimate light. The three beasts destroy Dante's hope of continuing his ascent up the steep hill by blocking his way and driving him back into the darkness. In that darkness someone appears to tell Dante that there is no such easy road to light as he is attempting. He must go by another way, the long journey through the grim darkness of the Inferno, into the breaking light of the Purgatorio, and finally up to the climactic vision of God in the Paradiso. This is the route of *The Divine Comedy*. "It is," as John Ciardi cogently states, "the painful descent into Hell—to the recognition of sin. It is the difficult ascent of Purgatory—to the renunciation of sin. Then only may Dante begin the soaring flight into Paradise, to the rapturous presence of God."[5]

Dante's first guide on his long journey is Virgil, who seems to be a complex combination of reason, philosophy, poetry, art and imagination. Perhaps Human Reason in its highest development, or Human Wisdom at its fullest, is one way of characterizing Virgil. Human Wisdom is one of Dante's guides in his journey toward God, but is not sufficient to take him into the very presence of God. Human Wisdom can awaken Dante's soul to a recognition of sin and a need for its renunciation, but an intervention of Divine Grace or Infinite Love, as represented by Beatrice, must take over Dante's soul before he can stand in the presence of a majestic and holy God.

As Dante's journey begins, he experiences not only a physical progression but a journey of profound inward consciousness. He sees the possibilities of sin within himself, the vileness of sin itself and the results of a life lived in sin. Similarly, he learns that no sinner is arbitrarily sent to Hell; all in Hell are there because of an obstinate will that chose its own destiny.

Hell is divided into nine concentric circles narrowing downward like an inverted cone, the sins becoming more heinous and the punishments more severe as the apex of the conical cavity is reached. Thus the law of Dante's Hell is the law of symbolic retribution: as one has sinned, so is he punished.

Virgil and Dante proceed to the Gate of Hell and on to Ante-Hell, or a vestibule of Hell, where the neutral souls reside. Refusing to take sides or make choices in life, they remain eternally unclassified. Their punishment is not so much torment as loathsome molestation: racing round and round pursuing a wavering banner that runs before them through the dirty air. As they run they are stung by insects. But their moral suffering appears far greater. Compassion and Justice turn aside from them. Heaven excludes them and they do not even belong in Hell. The first circle consists of Limbo where the unbaptized children and the virtuous pagans are placed. Virgil himself is a permanent inhabitant of this circle. Born without the light of Christ's revelation, the pagans are not physically tormented. Their pain is that they are without hope. After Circle One various classes of impenitent sinners are punished, the heinousness of the sin and the severity of the punishment increasing with the descent. The second through the fifth circles harbor those guilty of the sin of incontinence. Circle Two contains the lustful; Circle Three, the gluttonous; Circle Four, the avaricious and the prodigal; Circle Five, the slothful and the angry. Up to Circle Five Dante showed pity for those in Hell, but at this point he turns indignantly against those who, by a deliberate act of the will, chose cruelty. In Circle Six are the heretics; and the seventh circle, surrounded by the river Phlegethon, contains those guilty of violence: tyrants, murderers, suicides, squanderers, and those violent against God, nature or art. Circle Eight, or Malebolge, is a great circle of stone divided into ten concentric ditches wherein respectively are punished: (1) panderers and seducers, (2) flatterers, (3) simoniacs, (4) soothsayers and sorcerers, (5) grafters, (6) hypocrites, (7) thieves, (8) evil counselors, (9) sowers of discord, or scandalmongers and schismatics, and (10) alchemists, evil impersonators, false witnesses and various falsifiers.

The ninth circle contains the direst of sinners—those guilty of treachery. In the huge frozen area of the ninth circle the ice is divided into four concentric rings. Fixed in the ice, each according to his guilt, are punished, respectively, traitors to their (1) kindred, (2) country, (3) guests and hosts, and (4) masters or benefactors. Almost completely immersed in ice at the bottom of the fourth ring, at the farthest point from God, is Satan, who continuously grinds Judas, Brutus and Cassius in his teeth.

Through the law of symbolic retribution governing each sin, Dante's punishments "are chosen with a fantastic and gruesome ingenuity which reveals the richness, the dark pathos, and the almost pedantically precise concreteness of Dante's genius."[6] The punishments are enormously imaginative, each one based on a precise reflection of the degree of sin in question. And each one is designed to demonstrate the nature and horror of sin itself. The carnal, those who abandoned themselves to the tempest of their passion, are swept hither and thither by a great whirlwind; the heretics, those who taught that the soul dies with the body, are entombed in an eternal grave of fiery flames; the soothsayers, those who by forbidden arts attempted to look into the future, have their heads turned backward and are compelled to walk in that direction through all eternity—such examples of Dante's imaginative power "are not haphazard products of an irresponsible fantasy seeking to pile up horrors, but the work of a serious, inquiring mind which for each sin has chosen its appropriate punishment . . . and which owes the concreteness of its images to its conviction that its . . . choice is in conformity with the divine order."[7]

After the long journey through the concentric circles of Hell Dante begins the second stage of his journey in a new tone of hopefulness with the stars of Heaven before him. The sun rises to reveal the path of ascent up to the Mountain of Purgatory. Near the foot of the mountain is Ante-Purgatory, a region which contains souls waiting to be admitted to Purgatory. The souls waiting outside Purgatory include those who died as children and those who died excommunicated and—whether from negligence or because they died suddenly—repented only in death. Following his guide to the three steps of sincerity, contrition and love which lead to the gate of Purgatory, Dante pleads for admission to Purgatory proper; an angel carves on his forehead seven *P*'s, for the seven deadly sins, turns the gold and silver keys and admits Dante into Purgatory. As he climbs from terrace to terrace (and at each level a *P* is erased from Dante's brow), he sees examples of the seven deadly sins: pride, envy, wrath, sloth, prodigality (avarice), gluttony and lust; and of the corresponding virtues: humility, generosity, meekness, right love, right use, abstinence and chastity.

In addition to illustrations of the virtue corresponding to the vice punished, examples of persons guilty of specific sins are depicted. The suffering is, in most instances, of a nature opposed to the sin—the envious, with their eyes blinded to the beauties of the world are now totally dependent on one another; the gluttons, now emaciated images of thirst and starvation, waste away within view of food and drink. But all is not suffering in Purgatory: Hope prevails. As Dante wanders among the gluttonous, for example, one of them explains that he and his fellow-sufferers are obviously hungry and thirsty, but as their torment increases so also does their solace, since they thus crucify their appetites of the flesh, resulting in release from their sin.

Moving through the final terrace of Mount Purgatory, Dante comes to Eden. He now recognizes through the guidance of Virgil—Human Wisdom—the nature of sin and the need for renunciation. Standing in need of Revelation, he must now leave Virgil behind; Human Reason has gone as far as it is able. At first Dante weeps for Virgil and then for his own sin and faithlessness. Beatrice, symbol of Infinite Love or Revelation, bids Dante not to falter but to continue his journey.

Opening with a majestic statement on the nature of God as the All-Mover of the universe, the first canto of the *Paradiso* finds Dante with Beatrice at high noon, overwhelmed by the beauty of the order of the celestial spheres. Their conversation turns to man's need for God and to the enigma of those men who refuse to find their rest in Him. At this point Beatrice explains to Dante the wonderful gift of free will which God has entrusted to man; and as the conversation continues, Dante further learns the meaning and significance of redemption.

As Beatrice bears Dante aloft, he begins to see the glories and the inhabitants of the various planets. In the first three spheres, the Moon, Mercury and Venus, he beholds those who barely got into Heaven. On the following four planets are those exemplifying the four cardinal virtues: on the Sun, the wise; on Mars, the courageous warriors; on Jupiter, the just; and on Saturn, the contemplative spirits. In the Eighth Heaven, the sphere of Fixed Stars, Dante sees an intensely bright light shining from the triumphant Christ and observes a procession of those redeemed by Christ's sacrifice. Here, too, Dante is questioned by Peter, James, and John regarding his faith, hope and love. The Ninth Heaven is the Primum Mobile where motion, space and time begin. Here Dante gets a vision of the Angelic Choirs who are assigned to the various Heavens from the first through the ninth: Archangels, Principalities, Powers, Virtues, Dominions, Thrones, Cherubim and Seraphim.

Out beyond time and space is the Empyrean, the heaven that is pure light. At Beatrice's request St. Bernard appears to direct Dante in the final stages of his spiritual pilgrimage. He does not explain or teach as Virgil and Beatrice have done, but prays with and for Dante. Through the intercession of St. Bernard, as well as Beatrice and other redeemed ones, Dante finally is enabled to gaze directly upon God. The journey is now complete. The poet, thus having found his way to God, is so moved by what he beholds that he prays for grace to be able to speak of what he sees, that generations "yet unborn" may catch some glimpse of the sublime vision.

Seven centuries of study and scholarship have not exhausted all that Dante saw in the "sublime vision" or in any part of his long journey. But the more one studies this monumental poem the more he is unwilling to contradict the judgment of T. S. Eliot that "the majority of poems one outgrows and outlives. . . . Dante's is one of those which one can only hope to grow up to at the end of life."[8]

TROPES AND EARLY RELIGIOUS "DRAMA"

Within the early Christian church, in its religious functions and in its dramatization of the liturgy, religious drama began to appear. Exactly when religious drama originated is difficult to decide. Hardin Craig insists that its origin is simple, although when the story is told it often seems as if it were a matter of great complexity. "It happens," says Craig, "that at a definite time and place there came together in an exercise of representative art three factors that are the constituents of drama; namely, impersonation, action, and dialogue."[9]

Further clarifying his point of view, Craig states:

> Dialogue is provided for in the liturgy in the greatest abundance, since, not only in antiphones and responses but in recitals of all sorts, singing was responsive—between a single leader and a chorus, between two parts of a divided chorus, or between any parts or groupings called for by the liturgy. There was of course also much symbolic action, gesture, and movement, and there were also elements of impersonation, inherent in vestments and in the allocation of parts or roles in the service.[10]

It would seem then that religious drama began with the tropes, which were alternating chants or amplifications of passages in the liturgy. The tropes usually assumed to have originated in the ninth century were produced and widely used until the sixteenth century. Among the many tropes extant the oldest is the *Quem Quaeritis* which tells the story of the visit of the three Marys to the sepulcher and their dialogue with the angel on Easter morning.

From the liturgical drama—and particularly the *Quem Quaeritis* trope—it is likely that miracle or mystery plays developed.

These plays dramatized episodes from the Bible or events in the life of a martyr or saint. With a clearly didactic purpose, the miracle or mystery play gave special emphasis to the theme of the inevitability of punishment for all who revolted against God.

At some point in the thirteenth or fourteenth century the subject matter of the plays began to extend beyond episodes from the Bible or events in the saints' lives, and the performances moved out of the church into the churchyard and finally across the street into the marketplace, where they were taken over by the guilds. The plays grew into cycles and an entire cycle of these miracle plays (English literature does not make a distinction between a miracle and mystery play; French literature does) would be performed by various guilds in a town on a given holy day. Literary history often asserts the earliest surviving English miracle play to be *The Harrowing of Hell*, which dramatized the subject of Christ's descent into hell. Writers of miracle plays sometimes allowed elements of comedy to invade the religious stories. In the *Second Shepherd's Play*, for instance, the main plot deals with the birth of Christ, but there is a subplot connected with the theft of a sheep.

Around the fourteenth century there emerged a new type of play in which the characters were abstract personages and the central theme was usually the struggle between Vice and Virtue, or between Satan and God, for the possession of the human soul. Little is known of the origins of these so-called morality plays, but it seems probable that they arose independently of the miracle plays. Usually performed by professional actors, the morality plays were designed, as the name connotes, to present some moral and religious message. Perhaps the most popular of the morality plays in English literature is *Everyman*, believed to have been composed in the fifteenth century. It depicts simply a contest for the soul of "Everyman," a representative of all mankind. The play contains a number of humorous passages, but it also makes clear the serious fact that God sends death as a messenger to Everyman, warning that there comes a day when the records of man's life are closed. He may beg for a postponement of death, but the pleas cannot be granted. He may implore others to go with him, but only the "garments of contrition" accompanied by enduring good deeds are able to go with him into the grave. *Everyman*, with its personified abstractions set in a framework of allegory, is clearly didactic, but its emphasis is without question on the morals themselves rather than upon an Authority or Reality that gives significance to the morals.

LITERATURE OF THE MYSTICS

The fourteenth century was peculiarly rich in literature written by mystics. This is the period of such eminent mystical writers as Eckhardt, Tauler, Suso, Ruysbroeck on the Continent, and the century of Richard Rolle, Walter Hilton, Juliana of Norwich, and the unknown author of *The Cloud of Unknowing* in England.

The word "mystic" is perhaps one of the most ambiguous and misunderstood terms to be found in a study of religious literature. Some doubt that it conveys any sense of precision. But scholars of mysticism help provide guidelines for placing the term in perspective.

Evelyn Underhill, a prominent scholar of English mysticism, says that the Christian mystic is one "for whom God and Christ are not merely objects of belief, but living facts . . . known at first-hand; and mysticism for him becomes, in so far as he responds to its demands, a life based on the conscious communion with God." She further holds that the mystics are the greatest of all teachers of the privilege and duty of prayer, and "of that deeper communion to which disciplined prayer can lead."[11]

Students of mysticism pay great tribute to the fourteenth century English mystic, Walter Hilton, and students of literature are impressed with the literary power of his famous work, *The Scale of Perfection.* Using the image of the ladder and depicting spiritual growth in terms of two metaphors: a "re-forming" of the lost divine image of the soul, and a journey or pilgrimage to Jerusalem, Hilton presents the need for man to take one step at a time on the ladder in his development of a deep, satisfying Christian experience. This gradual ascent takes place, according to Hilton, as God gives grace and as man arduously strives.

A mystical writer on the Continent and author of a fifteenth century religious classic deserving special study is Thomas à Kempis.

THOMAS À KEMPIS (*c.* 1380-1471)

In one of his earliest portraits Thomas à Kempis is seen in a monastic cell holding a book, with an open volume on the floor bearing an inscription something like this: In all things have I sought rest, but nowhere have I found it save in a nook with a book. Although he spent seventy years in a monastery and loved a good book and a quiet corner, during all this time he was, nevertheless, a busy copyist, author, teacher and preacher. Born in the village of Kempen in Rhenish Prussia, he entered the monastery of Saint Agnes near Zwolle in 1400 and began preparation for his life as a monk with the Brothers of the Common Life movement.

THE IMITATION OF CHRIST (1480)

The Imitation of Christ grew out of Thomas à Kempis' experiences in ascetic living and his genuine desire to give spiritual counsel to his fellows. Besides the intrinsic qualities of the book itself, it gained fame for many years because of the numerous, and often violent, controversies concerning its authorship. But that contest is another study.

When a reader turns to the *Imitation of Christ,* perhaps he is first impressed by its utter simplicity. Yet the book is treasured by the trained as well as the untrained. It has crossed over all barriers of creed and language. Auguste Comte says of it: "It is an inextinguishable treasure of true wisdom," adding that the "poem of the 'Imitation' has been for years one of the principal daily sources of nourishment and consolation to my soul." Matthew Arnold calls it "the most exquisite document after the New Testament," and George Eliot declares, "It works miracles to this day."

As the title indicates, the central thesis of the book is that the Christian should strive to imitate, insofar as it is humanly possible, the life of Jesus Christ. To achieve this means he must concentrate on the inner life and its growth and develop less and less affection for the things of the world. The author's preoccupation with the inner life may be captured from a glance at subtitles of three of the four books of the *Imitation of Christ*: "Admonitions, Useful for a Spiritual Life," "Admonitions Tending to Things Eternal" and "Of Inward Consolation." And certainly the fourth book with its subtitle, "Concerning the Sacrament," reminds the reader that Thomas à Kempis' central thesis remains unchanged, for the emphasis is still on man's need for union with God.

Book I presents methods whereby the inner life may develop. The desires of the flesh must be resisted and resistance must be followed by humility. Asserting that speech must be carefully watched and guarded, Thomas à Kempis further avers that peace of soul comes through minding one's own business and constantly looking to eternal rather than temporal matters. Adversities are good for one's inner growth, for they cause one to turn to God rather than to man. Temptations, too, may contribute to the development of man's inner life if they are fraught with the weapons of patience and humility.

In the second book the concept of the reality of a developed inner life is brought home by a series of admonitions which teach the higher virtues. Humility is particularly enjoined, but humility must be accompanied by simplicity and purity. Along with simplicity and purity must go self-criticism and the avoidance of criticizing others. If an individual genuinely desires true inner peace, he must be willing to pay the price of obedience and endurance and to regard everything as worthless in this world in comparison with a life filled with deep love for God. Anything whatever that will draw attention to oneself and promote self-interest should be avoided, for true love for Christ is free from self-love. Besides, self-interest can lead to pride, and pride is foreign to a life of self-denial and crossbearing.

Thomas à Kempis appreciates the absurdity of his position in the world's eyes. "It is not according to man's inclination to bear the Cross . . . to flee honours . . . to endure adversities . . . to desire no prosperity in this world." But the aim of the dedicated man should be to recognize a "second nature" which is attuned to the eternal world.

Book III, the longest of the four and sometimes published separately, continues the emphasis upon the need for the development of higher virtues in the inner life. Stressing also the necessity for one to rest in God and to know the consolation of inner peace, Thomas à Kempis states four things that will bring true liberty and peace: doing the will of another rather than one's own; choosing to have "less rather than more" material possessions; seeking always the lowest place; and praying that God's will may be wholly fulfilled in us. Combined with these injunctions there is the reiterated reminder that love for self definitely hinders attainment of inner peace, and man should constantly pray for a clean heart and heavenly wisdom. The final book is an exhortation on the spiritual significance of the sacrament of Holy Communion.

The *Imitation of Christ* reveals the author's formula for living a life that imitates the model given in the person of Christ. Obedience, humility, contrition, and self-discipline are all essential if one is seriously interested in living a life that imitates Christ.

Simplicity and austerity characterize the style of the terse, epigrammatic sentences of Thomas à Kempis' *Imitation of Christ*. A typical statement illustrative of his style is: "Be not therefore exalted in thine own mind for any art or science which thou knowest, but rather let the knowledge given thee, make thee more humble and cautious."

Though admired for his numerous injunctions, Thomas à Kempis' artistic power has not been ignored. De Montmorency says, "The artist . . . was an author of the highest rank, and he built his work, sentence by sentence, with an indefinable skill, with a constructive genius that defied analysis."[12]

OTHER WORKS

Although there continued to be other writings in the mystical tradition, devotional guidebooks and collections of prayers throughout the sixteenth century, the great bulk of literature was man-oriented. With the spread of the Renaissance and the influence of humanism, some of the literature of the fourteenth, and even more of the writings of the fifteenth and sixteenth centuries, placed great stress upon the freedom and dignity of man as an individual and as a human being created only for this world. The humanists continued to venerate the study of the Church Fathers, but the heart of their thinking lay in the emphasis placed on Greek philosophies and secular learning in general. Nevertheless, interest in religion and in producing religious writings was still intense.

Provoked by the proclamation of Martin Luther's ninety-five theses in 1517 and the coming of the Reformation, the sixteenth century produced a number of distinctively religious—primarily theological and polemical—works from such men of stature as Luther, Zwingli, Calvin and William Tyndale, who worked on a translation of the Bible into English.

After Tyndale completed on the Continent a translation of the New Testament, copies of it were smuggled into England, but were then seized by the church authorities and burned. He issued a revised edition in 1534 and later translated the Pentateuch and the book of Jonah. The work of completing the translation of the Scriptures was carried out by Miles Coverdale. Hardin Craig refers to Coverdale's work as only "fair scholarship," but asserts that Tyndale's translation is important in English literature and "was the shaping element in the noble prose of the Authorized Version of 1611."[13]

The Book of Common Prayer also appeared in the sixteenth century. Dating from 1549, during the reign of Edward VI, the work is credited primarily to Thomas Cranmer. In 1560 the Geneva Bible was published in England and went through one hundred sixty editions in fifty years, "becoming the English Bible in current use until the making of the Authorized or King James Version in 1611."[14]

Another sixteenth century work was John Foxe's *Book of Martyrs* which gives a history of martyrdom from the beginning of Christianity. His stories of the Oxford Martyrs—Latimer, Ridley and Cranmer—are among his most famous accounts.

The Counter-Reformation of the Catholic Church exercised influence on a number of writers and translators. A stream of controversial literature came from the press of the college at Douay, later at Rheims. The college, founded by an English Catholic trained at Oxford, was also responsible for the Douay Bible.

Another Englishman who participated in the Counter-Reformation, Robert Southwell, wrote a few poems of some literary merit. "The Burning Babe," a Christmas carol much admired by the seventeenth century author, Ben Jonson, and "St. Peter's Complaint" are among Southwell's best known poems.

The sixteenth century with its crosscurrents of influence produced other writers that appropriated in their own distinctively artistic ways various branches of thought and art. In referring, for example, to Edmund Spenser, Hardin Craig says: "To Renaissance forms grounded on Plato, Aristotle, and the Latin poets Spenser brought a sense of historical continuity—romance, religion, chivalry, magic, and allegory."[15] Although classical and humanistic influences are interwoven with Arthurian romantic elements in his poem the *Faerie Queene*, Spenser also adds a strong Christian element. One illustration of the latter in the first book is the Red Cross Knight, who stands for holiness. The story concerns his going with Una, or Truth, to slay the dragon, Error, which is destroying her father's domain. The united power of Truth and Holiness is essential in the overthrow of Error.

Certainly William Shakespeare, whose work continues into the seventeenth century, does not appropriate exclusively the humanistic aspects of his era. Although humanism is strong in his writings, Christian implications are also frequently present. In his well-known tragedy, *Macbeth*, for instance, Shakespeare places responsibility squarely on Macbeth. Macbeth makes a choice: he chooses to murder his king, who is also his guest, and he must face the consequences of his choice. Acknowledging his league with evil, he speaks of "mine eternal jewel/Given to the common enemy of man." The consequences of the compact deepen as Macbeth realizes that justice and punishment cannot be evaded. Although Macbeth possesses a fear of being detected by his fellowmen, he also seems to have another deep concern—particularly as he contemplates murdering his king. G. I. Duthie, commenting on this "other" preoccupation, says of one of Macbeth's early soliloquies (Act I, vii): "He speaks, of 'angels, trumpet-tongued' pleading against 'the deep damnation' of Duncan's 'taking-off.' And he speaks of Pity . . . blowing 'the horrid deed in every eye.' The imagery is religious—apocalyptic. . . . he is very much preoccupied with the life to come . . . fundamentally he believes in the law of God."[16] Admittedly, the quoted statement and scores of others similar in nature which could be cited, may give little support for a Christian *Weltanschauung* for William Shakespeare. But the point is that the famous dramatist and poet was not completely engulfed by the humanistic spirit permeating his world.

In the latter years of the sixteenth century a number of religious writers, to be discussed in the following chapter, began their careers, but the bulk of their writing was done in the seventeenth century.

CHAPTER 2

The Seventeenth Century

THE SEVENTEENTH CENTURY was a crucial one in the history of Western thought. It was a time of conflict: forces were molding the modern spirit, while there was irresistible pressure to preserve traditional ideas. It saw the beginnings and growth of rationalism, which was partly responsible for introducing the concept of a mechanistic universe and turning thought toward psychological investigation. The century also saw the development of the scientific spirit which evoked a new interest in the study of human experience and the gathering of experimental data. Theology no longer set limits to a thinker's investigation nor dictated the conclusions at which he must arrive. On the other hand, there was Puritanism which had far-reaching influence in the world of political theory as well as in the realm of morals.

The Puritans were not interested in countering every aspect of the new rationalistic and scientific spirit of the century, nor were they at all interested in preserving many of the practices associated with traditional theology. They, too, were concerned with the study of the universe, but they believed that God created it as a unified, ordered, purposeful whole and that all aspects of it had meaning only within this totality. They further believed that man was free to investigate and explore wherever his inquiring mind led him, but they resisted the pressure to throw off all authority. To them the Bible was the revelation of infinite wisdom and should be revered as such. And rather than this belief hampering man's intellectual pursuits, they felt it gave learning a frame of reference. Also in the seventeenth century, particularly in the established Church of England, numbers of well-educated clergymen, who were also writers, demonstrated an awareness of the inroads of the new thought and spirit, recognized the positive contributions, yet expressed their firm belief that religious truth and values must be preserved. Authors in the Anglican and Puritan traditions—and many of the early Puritans were Anglicans—constitute the major bulk of seventeenth century religious literature.

JOHN DONNE (1572-1631)

John Donne, English preacher, poet and scholar, requires of his readers a knowledge of seventeenth century theology, philosophy, science and just about every other learned subject of the period. And this need is intensified because "Donne talks directly out of his intellectual and emotional situation. He does not view his subjects from the outside, talk about them, and criticize them, but presents with singular lack of restraint the very content of his own mind."[1]

Donne's father was a London ironmonger, and his mother was the daughter of dramatist John Heywood. Donne's family was solidly Roman Catholic, and the decision over what form his own faith should take became an intense struggle in his early life.

Donne attended both Oxford and Cambridge and entered as a law student at Lincoln's Inn. In 1598 he became secretary to Sir Thomas Egerton, Lord Keeper of the Great Seal, but lost his job because in 1601 he eloped with Anne More, niece of his patron's wife, and his indignant father-in-law had him dismissed from Egerton's service. For several years Donne underwent poverty and indefinite employment. In 1615 he took orders in the Anglican Church, after which he held some minor preferments, and from 1621 until his death in 1631 he was Dean of St. Paul's Cathedral. During that time he became known as one of the greatest—if not the greatest—of English preachers.

DEVOTIONS UPON EMERGENT OCCASIONS (1624)

Probably one of the most widely read of his prose works, Donne's *Devotions* is divided into twenty-three portions, and each portion represents a stage of the author's illness during the winter of 1623-24. Every mental and physical characteristic of the disease is analyzed in detail. The work begins with a description of the first stages of the illness and moves on through the periods of the doctor's coming, the physician's consultation with other physicians and their various efforts to "purge" the disease. By

Section XIII it is evident that the treatments are not successful. The crisis comes, and Sections XVI through XVIII contain the famous passages on death, meditations written as the bells of a nearby church toll. By Section XIX the crisis is over, and the remaining portions deal with treatments given by the doctors. The work concludes with caution against a relapse.

Donne's work is filled with discoveries on the relative importance of various parts of his anatomy and with lengthy discussions of quaint medieval practices used by his doctors. But one does not read long before he recognizes that Donne is not preoccupied with seventeenth century medical lore. Through his many allusions and analogies, Donne extends the work from physical illness to the illness of the state and to the general human condition. In Section XII, for example, Donne tells of the doctor's assumption that "vapors" had caused his illness and the consequent application of pigeons to his feet in order to draw the "vapors" from his head. Reflecting for several lines on the cause of the "vapors," and comparing his personal problems to the illness of the state, he goes on to find religious significance in the quaint "pigeon-purging" remedy used by his doctors. To Donne this remedy is simply and significantly a symbol of the visitation of the Spirit, who descended in the form of a dove that the vapors of sin might be purged and trod underfoot.

Throughout the *Devotions*, Donne does not doubt the reality of his own physical illness, but he uses it as a point of departure for reflection on a variety of subjects. In Section X he speaks of physical illness as representing sin. The doctors find Donne's disease one that steals on "insensibly," and the author uses this to show how Satan sneaks up and attacks an individual when he least suspects danger. In addition to the discourse on sin, one is able to follow the wrestlings of Donne's mind and spirit as he grapples with other topics that concerned him most intimately, like repentance, death, resurrection, judgment and the immortality of the soul. And surely his eloquent reflections on death—particularly in Sections XVI through XVIII—aid in explaining why the *Devotions* is a classic in religious literature.

Lying on his sickbed, Donne hears through the window the tolling of bells at the funeral of a neighbor, which provides the occasion for what is undoubtedly the most popularly known and most impressive passage of the *Devotions*. He begins: "Here the bells can scarce solemnize the funeral of any person, but that I knew him, or knew that he was my neighbor: we dwelt in houses near to one another before, but now he is gone into that house into which I must follow him." Donne realizes that it might well have been his death for which those bells are tolling.

As the bells continue to toll, Donne turns to the world of books and scholarship (a world he knew well) for a metaphor to show how mankind is united. Donne says, "All mankind is of one author, and is of one volume; when one man dies, one chapter is not torn out of the book, but translated into a better language; and every chapter must be so translated; God employs several translators; some pieces are translated by age, some by sickness, some by war, some by justice; but God's hand is in every translation, and his hand shall bind up all our scattered leaves again for that library where every book shall lie open to one another."

Donne then returns not only to the metaphor of the bell but also to the geographical image of the world (an image he often used in his writings) to conclude his significant statement on the unity of mankind in one of the most memorable passages of the entire work: "No man is an island, entire of itself; every man is a piece of the continent, a part of the main. If a clod be washed away by the sea, Europe is the less . . . as well as if a manor of thy friends' or of thine own were; any man's death diminishes me, because I am involved in mankind, and therefore never send to know for whom the bell tolls; it tolls for thee."

These passages just quoted are of great beauty, and Donne uses his metaphors and images to release a strong argument. As K. W. Gransden says: "There is nothing of . . . romantic humanism in Donne's affirmation, 'I am involved in mankind.' Donne is no philanthropic Victorian 'liberal humanist': he does not say 'all men are brother,' which means 'if everyone was kind, tolerant, etc. . . . everything would be all right.' Donne . . . gives us his all important logical *reasons* for claiming to be involved in mankind. It is that 'all mankind is of one author.' "[2]

Donne's nearly fatal illness brought numerous reflections on death in his *Devotions,* yet he does not seem to fear it. He sees it as part of God's plan to bring an end to man's sinning. He prays: "Let this prayer therefore, O my God, be as my last gasp . . . that if this be the hour of my transmigration I may die the death of a sinner, drowned in my sins, in the blood of Thy son. And if I live longer, yet I may now die the death of the righteous, die to sin, which death is a resurrection to a new life. . . ."

The *Devotions*, dominantly introspective, possesses an extraordinary objectivity, for those communions of Donne's soul with God exemplify his great power of analysis and analogy which he used so often in his literary art.

Though not as widely read as the *Devotions*, the *Essays in Divinity* is another of Donne's major works. It is sometimes suggested that *Essays* is important as a solid balance to the more personal, self-revelatory *Devotions*. The *Essays in Divinity*, written at some point during the five years before Donne's ordination, is an attempt to set down the meaning of some large, basic Christian concepts and to clarify his own views on the Christian faith. The work shows a brilliant mind working with theological problems in scholarly, closely knit arguments, and the *Essays* is much more central to his position as a theologian than the artistic *Devotions*.

SERMONS

Donne's literary works during the last sixteen years of his life were almost exclusively sermons. More than one hundred and fifty of his sermons were published during the seventeenth century. Donne's sermons are not merely expository in nature, but fuse the rhetorical, logical, and poetical, a fusion essential to the formation of the greatest sermons and the achievement of the greatest art. Says Donne: "He who brings any collateral respect to a sermon, loses the blessing of God's ordinance in the sermon: he hears but the logic, or the rhetoric, or the poetry of the sermon, but the sermon of the sermon he hears not."

Donne's sermons cover a wide range of subjects. The trinity, the incarnation, creation, the doctrine of man (and how man knows God), the sacraments, prayer, repentance, redemption, worship, vocations, callings, death, resurrection and the relationship between faith and reason are among the topics which preoccupied Donne's attention as a builder of sermons and a preacher. In his sermons he draws images, references, examples, illustrations, paradoxes and allusions from virtually all possible fields of knowledge. Recondite and farfetched though some of his images may seem, Donne, a thoroughly conscious artist, knew what he was doing and what he wanted to achieve. He felt that the sermon, as an art form that makes use of language and secular and scriptural learning, should be preached for the glory of God and for the intellectual and spiritual growth of the parishioners.

Believing that it behooves a preacher-artist to prepare "a pattern to work by" or "an example to proceed by," Donne developed an idea or "pattern" of sermonizing. "From the meanest artificer, through the wisest philosopher, to God himself," says Donne, "all that is well done or wisely undertaken, is undertaken and done according to preconceptions, foreimaginations, designs, and patterns proposed to ourselves beforehand . . . God does nothing, man does nothing well . . . without this recourse to preconceptions, predeliberations." Consequently Donne's sermons, which are models of clarity, demonstrate an organization of mathematical precision. Beginning with the statement of the text, Donne usually examines it from various angles, elucidates it, shows the implications for daily living, and finally brings together aspects of the sermon in a succinct summary.

A study of one of Donne's sermons will show something of his power as a preacher and a skillful master of prose. On Easter Day, 1628, Donne preached at St. Paul's on I Corinthians 13:12: "For now we see through a glass, darkly; but then face to face: now I know in part; but then shall I know even as also I am known." As Donne probes the text, he unfolds a clear picture of how man may know God. There are four stages in ascending order in man's knowledge of God, with each stage symbolized by a particular kind of light—the light of reason, the light of faith, the light of glory and the Light which is God. Two of these stages occur while man is still on earth and the other two stages, which bring a full and complete knowledge of God, occur after he arrives in heaven.

As man observes the phenomenal world, the light of his reason shows him that there is a God. The whole of creation is a medium through which God's being is revealed, and the light which enables one to see God in His works is the light of reason. But the light of reason is not sufficient for man even to "know in part"; he needs the light of faith. Donne insists upon an understanding, intelligent faith. How does man get this understanding faith? From a knowledge of the Scriptures *in the church*, is Donne's staunch belief. To Donne it was the responsibility of the minister to explicate clearly the Scriptures so that individuals would have the occasion to develop an intelligent faith. The church, too, was very important to him as a holy place, with sermonizing as the central part of the service. He was by no means opposed to liturgy, but he believed that the significance of the liturgy should be clear to those in attendance at the church services.

Donne stresses that through reason one "sees" God and through faith one "knows in part," but not until man passes from life here into the presence of God can he fully know Him. Perhaps for the benefit of the mystics of his day, he admits that there may be "moments of radiant insight," but he reminds all that such insights are transitory. Donne does not necessarily question or minimize the mystical insight, but his mind is essentially not a mystical one.

The third light is the light of glory which man will see and know when he passes from mortality into immortality. The glorious gospel is but a "star of least magnitude" in comparison with this light which enables man to see God face to face. But to see is not to know Him "as we are known" by Him. In the final stage there is ultimate revelation of God Himself. This light is not a "light which is His, but a light which is He." "God alone is all," writes Donne, "in all the former there was a place, and a means, and a light; here, for this perfect knowledge of God, God is all those." Man shall know even as he is known when he arrives at the final light after the step-by-step, gradual ascent through the various lights whereby one knows God. Then shall man completely know God.

Even though Donne's sermons are filled with theological insight and religious discovery, perhaps it is true that it will not be for these that his "sermons will be finally valued, but for their revelation of a singularly broad and alive spirit, wrestling with some of the enduring problems of the inner life."[3] As prose, too, the sermons contain the seeds of permanency, for as "knotty and ingenious and involved as are many passages in their text-girded pages, they yet afford rich and beautiful passages of sheer prose-poetry almost beyond number."[4]

SELECTED RELIGIOUS POEMS

John Donne is often referred to as the father of metaphysical poetry. The "metaphysical school" of poetry was a group of writers employing similar form in their poems. Firmly intellectual and analytical in structure, metaphysical poetry reveals deeply personal and provocative thoughts on a variety of subjects, but with topics such as death, love and religious devotion receiving concentrated attention. Particularly striking is the imagery used by the metaphysical poets, who are especially fond of sudden turns of thought, farfetched metaphors, multiple analogies and plays on words.

John Donne is the author of many unique poems, but as Helen White says, "the religious verse of John Donne owes very little of its distinction to either its quantity or its variety."[5] Like any good poet, Donne selects, combines, and reorganizes experiences—often intensely personal ones—and casts them into a literary form in which others can participate.

Satyre III

What form shall my faith take? is obviously the question with which Donne is wrestling in this poem. Is the expression of one's faith found in the Roman Church, the established Church of England, any church, no church? "On a huge hill, / Cragged, and steep, Truth stands, and hee that will / Reach her, about must, and about must goe," says Donne. He lays the onus squarely on the individual to seek, to find and to decide for himself, because of his freedom to choose. Man is to know God and not to substitute his own beliefs for a knowledge of God. And Donne cautions that the laws of man are the canons of many dogmatic religionists rather than the laws of God. Man becomes guilty of idolatry in dedicating himself to such beliefs rather than to God Himself.

Holy Sonnets (Selected)

Number I

Death should not be proud, for it holds no terrors: "One short sleepe past, wee wake eternally / And death shall be no more; death, thou shalt die." Death conquers death, for it is a gate to life.

Number XIV

"Batter my heart, three person'd God" cries Donne as he passionately argues his powerlessness to escape Satan's thralldom unless Christ as a Victor-lover releases him. Donne says, ". . . for I / Except you enthrall me, never shall be free, / Nor ever chaste, except you ravish me."

La Corona Sonnets

The "La Corona" cycle, a set of seven linked sonnets, is generally included among the *Holy Sonnets*, but the "La Corona" is less personal than most of the *Holy Sonnets*. These sonnets are formal compositions on the "great traditional devotional themes, resembling some noble series of full page miniatures of the Life of Christ at the beginning of a medieval psalter."[6] The first line of each sonnet is the same as the last line of the preceding sonnet, while the last line of the final sonnet is the same as the first line of Sonnet One.

Good Friday: 1613 Riding Westward

This is the last of Donne's religious poems written before his ordination, and may be considered as an arrow pointing toward the target of his hymns.

It is an intimately personal poem that contains within its metaphysical conceits and striking paradoxes a stirring depiction of what it meant to Donne for Christ to die:

> Hence is't that I am carried towards the West
> This day, when my soul's form bends towards the East.
> There I should see a Sun, by rising set,
> And by that setting endless day beget;
> But that Christ on this cross did rise and fall,
> Sin had eternally benighted all.
> Yet dare I almost be glad I do not see
> That spectacle of too much weight for me.
> Who sees God's face, that is self like, must die:
> What a death were it then to see God die?
> It made His footstool crack and the sun wink.
> Could I behold those hands which span the Poles,
> And tune all spheres at once, pierc'd with those holes?
> Could I behold that endless height which is
> Zenith to us, and our Antipodes,
> The seat of all our souls, if not of His
> Made dirt of dust, or that flesh which was worn
> By God, for His apparel, ragg'd and torn?

This reflection on the suffering of Christ is followed by a cry to the Saviour to restore His image in Donne:

O Saviour, as Thou hang'st upon the tree,
I turn my back to Thee, but to receive
Corrections, till Thy mercies bid Thee leave.
O think me worth Thine anger, punish me,
Burn off my rusts and my deformity;
Restore Thine image so much, by Thy grace,
That Thou may'st know me, and I'll turn my face.

That Christ died for man is not simply a theological concept or a tremendous historical event to John Donne. It is also something deeply personal for this seventeenth century poet.

A Hymn to God the Father

Donne asks God for forgiveness of his sins in this hymn. Punning on his name (and probably on the name of his wife, Anne More), he states: "When thou hast done, thou hast not done / For, I have more." He acknowledges his sin of fear and invokes as a guarantee against this fear a promise from God:

But swear by thy self, that at my death thy son
 Shall shine as he shines now, and heretofore,
And having done that, Thou hast done,
 I fear no more.

Hymn to God My God, In My Sickness

Donne apparently conceived of this hymn—actually an analytical sermon addressed to his own soul—as a deathbed poem. Some scholars believe the poem was written in 1631 when Donne thought he was dying; others date the work in 1623 during the severe illness of Donne referred to in the *Devotions*.

Heaven is harmony, and Donne's soul must be brought to internal harmony; it must be tuned before death in order to be prepared for the harmony of heaven. Comparing his physicians to cosmographers, Donne says that as they study the "map" of his body, their diagnosis is that he is going to die. But Donne rejoices that through the "straits" of his fever he will see his "West" for "As West and East / In all flat maps (and I am one) are one / So death doth touch the Resurrection." Donne brings the poem to a close with a potent, authoritative, yet paradoxical statement undoubtedly based on Psalm 146:8 when he says: "Therefore that he may raise the Lord throws down."

GEORGE HERBERT (1593-1633)

Herbert had already written some poetry when he received his degree from Cambridge in 1612. In 1614 he became a fellow of Trinity College, Cambridge, and in 1616 he took his Master of Arts degree. He was appointed reader in rhetoric in 1618. Although Herbert was apparently preparing for a career in the church, there is evidence that he was by no means indifferent to a promising secular career. From the fall of 1618 he worked hard to secure the post of Public Orator at Cambridge, and in 1620 he realized his ambition. Herbert undoubtedly used the opportunities of his office to push his fortunes with the king and the court. Precisely what ended his career is not easy to determine. A series of deaths including his mother's, the influence of John Donne, the awareness of the passing of time, combined with the remembrance of the work he knew he was born to do are sometimes given as explanations for Herbert's leaving his post as Public Orator and making up his mind to enter into Holy Orders. The remaining years of his life were spent in serving the small country parish at Bemerton. In addition to his pastoral duties, Herbert worked hard on translating a few works, writing and revising his poems and preparing a guidance manual for country parsons.

George Herbert was deeply concerned over the lack of poetry on religious themes. He was not necessarily opposed to poetry on secular themes, but he believed that it should not monopolize the field. Before his death he destroyed his secular poems and left for posterity only his body of religious poetry. Nicholas Ferrar, founder of the religious community Little Gidding and an intimate friend of Herbert, was responsible for the publication in 1633 of his collected religious poems, *The Temple.*

Herbert's poetry reflects a profound sense of the immanence of God as well as a very personal sense of God's yearning for man. It also reveals the characteristic qualities of the metaphysical poem: the firmness of intellectual structure in the poem as a whole, the precision of phrasing and the striking turns of thought or expression. There is conflict in his poetry, yet calm trust; there is disturbed speculation, yet simple faith. Using a remarkable number of stanzaic forms, Herbert rarely repeats himself, except of course, when he employs the sonnet or some other conventional form. There was for Herbert no one architectural pattern. A new subject or a new experience had to be cast in a new form.

"THE PULLEY"

The pulley is an emblem of the restlessness of man. God has given every blessing except rest to man, and if man will not come to God through other means, perhaps his weariness will bring him to God's breast.

"THE COLLAR"

In a stanzaic form, emblematic of a disordered life, the poet rebels against the apparent restrictions and the possible sterility of his life, until the struggle is resolved with a realization of a new relationship. As he rants and raves the frenzy deepens, and the line of argument falls from the humanistic to the materialistic and opportunistic level. Then comes the powerful awareness that quiets the tensions of rebellion. Herbert describes it in this manner:

> But as I rav'd and grew more fierce and wild
>> At every word,
> Methought I heard one calling, "Childe,"
> And I replied, "My Lord."

"VIRTUE"

The poem is sometimes regarded "as the epitome of a life at peace with God." Emphasizing the transitoriness of things, a prominent seventeenth century theme, Herbert simply makes clear that the day, the rose and the spring all must die; but the virtuous soul like "seasoned timber, never gives" but lives forever.

"THE QUIP"

The seductions of the world such as beauty, money, glory, wit and conversation come to tempt the poet, but he tells the Lord to instruct these seducers that "I am thine." Then they shall have a sufficient answer.

"LOVE (III)"

The relationship between the soul and God is presented through a symbolic picture of a travel-worn guest receiving hospitality. Love, without being made to seem any less divine or personal, is given social graces to show the guest being welcomed to salvation, to the communion table, and into heaven.

Other Metaphysical Poets

Richard Crashaw (1613-1649) was born in London, the son of a Church of England clergyman, who was strongly anti-Roman. Crashaw, however, became a Roman Catholic and filled a number of his poems with ecstatic reflections on the lives of the saints and martyrs. His religious thought pivoted on the incarnation, which meant for him: "not that Christ had died for man to satisfy God's justice and redeem his elect, but that God should have come into the world, stooping his glory to the meanness of earth, adding to his ancient cares the littleness of human life."[7]

The wonder of the incarnation pervades the poem "Dear Bargain." It begins with a series of questions:

> Lord, what is man? Why should he cost thee
> So dear? What had his ruin lost thee?
> Lord, what is man? That Thou hast overbought
> So much a thing of naught?

As the poem continues the same questioning, awesome wonder penetrates Crashaw's meditative verse. Some of Crashaw's poetry reflects the influence of the Italian poet Marini, who composed what is generally considered the best verse of the seventeenth century Baroque poets. Marini introduced him to the rhetoric, ecstatic themes and sensuous imagery of Neo-Latin poetry. Under Marinistic influences Crashaw wrote a number of English epigrams on biblical themes as exercises in Baroque style. Yet the poem most characteristic of his absorption in Marini's poetry is "Saint Mary Magdalene," commonly called "The Weeper."

Crashaw's collection of sacred poetry, *Carmen Deo Nostro,* is filled with such intense passion that he is criticized for failing to construct poetry unified in its emotional or intellectual thrust.

Henry Vaughan (1622-1695) shows an indebtedness to George Herbert. Yet Vaughan is far more preoccupied with contemplation of nature and reminiscences of childhood than Herbert. Because some of Vaughan's poems are constructed around themes of nature and childhood, students of literature are quick to point out his relationship with the Romantic poet William Wordsworth.

The contemplation of nature for its own sake is not Vaughan's concern. To him the world is a living library; it is a "repository of instruction" through which God speaks to restless man.

The least of the creatures in God's created world has something to say to man, and Vaughan not only wants to *see* this creation, he wants to *hear* it. Man is that creature which God set above all of creation as the voice of the whole inarticulate universe. But although every other creature follows his ordained order, man rebelled against God and fell. To Henry Vaughan there is nothing passive anywhere in the universe, and each creature, however small, gives its message to the soul of man.[8] This thought pervades his poem, "Cock-Crowing," and gives further evidence, too, that his view of nature is intertwined with his view of man. Vaughan underscores this in "Corruption" when he reflects on man's fall and states that man, in his rebellion against God, betrayed not only himself but also the helpless created creatures of the world.

Vaughan's preoccupation with childhood is hard to decipher. At times he seems simply to desire for himself the simplicity and wonder of a little child; on the other hand, there is a deep wistfulness for the time when men lived in a closer relationship with God than in the unsettled seventeenth century.

Vaughan's poetry shows a thirst for knowing God fully and completely and reveals his discontent with the veil that separates him from God. His poem "Anguish" is undoubtedly one of the clearest expressions of the agony he endures because of the veil that hinders his full sense of God's presence. To Vaughan God is One who should be known and to whose will man should submit. While man is on this earth a God of divine providence is working out His will for man, as another poem, "Love and Discipline," declares.

Vaughan's poems contain some brilliant lines, but artistic strength, fully sustained throughout a poem, is a rare quality in his works.

Thomas Traherne (1634-1704) completes the line of seventeenth century metaphysical poets. Traherne's poetry stresses communion with God through the enjoyment and possession of the created world God gave to man. He contends that, unless man enjoys the world and esteems it as a gift from God, the end of creation is not attained and God is grieved. On occasion he pictures God as the Bridegroom who has built this world for man,

His bride; and nothing could displease God more than for man to reject the created world or not to accept it consciously as from Him. One of Traherne's better known poems is "Right Apprehension." But perhaps "The Wonder," which depicts a child's wonder at the body in which his soul dwells and the world into which he has been born, is the single poem which has brought Traherne greatest admiration.

As a poetic artist Traherne is not always successful. His poems lack development and growth; they often end where they started. But, in spite of some artistic defects, one of the greatest delights in reading Traherne is "the privilege of entering into the experience of a man to whom God and the Creation have come home in a peculiarly intimate and direct fashion."[9]

The poets of the metaphysical school not only show the power of the Christian faith in the shaping of poetry, they also point up the task of the Christian artist—to find the metaphor that will clothe and convey his vision.

SIR THOMAS BROWNE (1605-1682)

Sir Thomas Browne was educated at Westminster and at Oxford, and he later studied medicine on the Continent. After three years he came back to England and took up a medical practice at Norwich. When Browne was about thirty he drafted his religious biography, the *Religio Medici*. Many men of letters have helped spread the fame of Sir Thomas Browne. Among those who praise him are Poe, Melville, Pater, DeQuincey, Hazlitt, Coleridge, Lamb, Johnson and Lowell. Lowell paid great tribute to his style of writing and referred to Browne as "our most imaginative mind since Shakespeare." Writers of the contemporary world have likewise honored Browne, one of his chief admirers being C. S. Lewis, whose own arresting works artistically reassert the role of the Christian faith in life and literature.

When Browne's autobiography (or perhaps religious musings) first appeared, various interpretations were placed upon it. Some readers attacked Browne for being a Papist in disguise; others accused him of being an atheist; while some admiring Puritan editors suspected him of being an adherent of their position. One Quaker leader was so impressed with his contemplations on religion that he invited him to join the Society of Friends. It is perhaps not strange that various interpretations or misinterpretations are associated with Browne's work, for the plea for the in-dividual to follow his own conscience in matters of religion per-vades the book.

THE RELIGIO MEDICI (1642)

It is unwise to suggest that the *Religio Medici* made a strong contribution to religious thought, but it is just as unwise to ignore the work completely in a study of religious literature. Perhaps no more cogent statement regarding the book has been made than that of Basil Willey when he said that Browne was "pleading for religion in an age which was beginning to be dominated by science."[10]

In *Religio Medici* Browne sets down his opinion on a vast range of topics—the scientific search for truth, the relation between faith and reason, the creation of the world, the mystery and wonder of believing, the interpretation of the Bible and a multiplicity of other subjects.

Sir Thomas Browne opens his work by telling why he assumes the title of Christian and states clearly "not that I merely owe this title to the Font, my education, or climate wherein I was born, as being bred up either to confirm those principles my parents in-stilled into my unwary understanding, or by a general consent proceed in the religion of my country: But having, in my riper years, and confirmed judgment, seen and examined all, I find my-self obliged by the principles of Grace, and the law of mine own reason to embrace no other name but this. . . ."

After declaring that he bears the name Christian and that he is a member of the Church of England, he speaks of his toleration for other points of view. As his basis for belief he accepts the author-ity of two books which speak of "divinity": God's Word and the book of nature. Browne is troubled that many Christians fail to accept the validity of the revelation of nature, but he is just as concerned about many Christians' equally serious mistake: exam-ining the book of nature and forgetting God. He blatantly at-tacks the erroneous claims of science that would try to explain away the mystery of the created universe, but straightforwardly challenges the false theology that would deny man's right to honor the Creator God by exploring His handiwork. One does not see, however, in the *Religio Medici,* a serious attempt to bring about any integration between the two areas. Browne seems rather to divide his attention between the Bible and nature, observing the facts of nature with a Baconian empiricism, and at the same time rejoicing in his acceptance by faith of religious mysteries which are beyond the mind of man to explain. One must not fail to see, however, his succinct view of nature as "the art of God." Believing in a transcendent Creator who made the world in time and fashioned it as an artist fashions his materials, Browne is dissatisfied merely to study the mechanism. He sees that a study of the "how" and the "what" can tell him more about the "why"—the God who brought the world into being. But it still is not clearly evident that Browne is interested in an integrated approach to his findings. He proceeds with the basic assumption that this is God's world, and then goes on to point out certain observable facts about this world.

Browne thoroughly enjoys dwelling on the wonder and mystery of the Christian faith, and because of this he is sometimes labeled as hopelessly irrational. But his work shows that he is not a causally indifferent thinker, for he believes intensely that the world has a purpose and man a destiny and that God is in control of His created world. Yet the tone or the temper that envelops Browne's work is one of wonder. His famous phrase, "I love to lose myself in a mystery, to pursue my reason to an O altitudo" is typical of the spirit and atmosphere running throughout the *Religio Medici*.

Delighting in a faith that accepts miracles, Browne seriously cautions against believing in what people in the religious world of the seventeenth century label as miracles. He believes in the miracles recorded in Scripture, and that miracles could still occur in his age, for God's power is commensurate with His will. He glories that he was not one of those Israelites that passed through the Red Sea, nor one of Christ's "patients" on whom He wrought healing; for had he seen these miracles, he says, his faith would have been "thrust upon" him. " 'Tis an easy and necessary belief, to credit what our eye and sense have examined," and he is happy to be among those who "enjoy that greater blessing pronounced to all that believe and saw not."

The *Religio Medici* does not treat lightly the problems of belief. Browne had questions, and he could talk of doubts. But he refused to waste his life in the obsession of questions he could not answer, preferring to live in the reality of answers that he could not escape. Yet it is difficult to believe from his work that Browne really ever faced head-on some of the perplexities involved in real issues with which a mature faith must come to grips.

Though one may wish for more of a clear-cut *Weltanschauung* from his autobiography, there is truth in these discerning statements regarding Sir Thomas Browne and his *Religio Medici*:

> He proved that it is possible to be earnest about these important matters. . . . He gave its age what it badly needed: a fresh expression of an individual man's belief. . . . But the book would not have retained its unique place as a literary and religious classic unless it possessed qualities which appeal perennially to man. The engaging character of its author inevitably attracts all save the most doctrinaire minds. His curiosity, his charity toward others, his humility about himself, and his sense of the mystery and wonder of life makes him a rare and delightful companion.[11]

RICHARD BAXTER (1615-1691)

Richard Baxter has the reputation of being known during his lifetime as one of the foremost spokesmen of the Puritan party within the Church of England. A devout man with a powerful intellect, he was active in political affairs and was among the most renowned preachers in England. Apparently he considered his writings the most important contributions of his many-faceted life. His *Autobiography* combines many facts about his career and his world with a scrutinizing examination of the inner life. One of the distinctive qualities of Baxter's *Autobiography* is the manner in which it suggests "the significance to the growth of the soul of such factors as personal relationships, health, intellectual interests and the larger movements of history."[12]

THE SAINTS' EVERLASTING REST (1650)

Baxter maintains artistic unity by threading throughout the book the theme of the reward promised to the true Christian in the afterlife. He uses as his point of departure the verse of Scripture, "There remaineth therefore a rest to the people of God" (Heb. 4:9). Baxter relates the necessary signs of the true candidate for the rest, helps and hindrances toward a life fitting one for the rest, and finally the need to help others to become candidates for the rest. He stresses the value of meditation on the content and quality of the promised reward as a means of motivating and enabling the Christian to prepare for the promised rest. Nowhere does Baxter suggest that faith and reason are diametrically opposed. He urges an intelligent faith in considering the "rest" for the children of God. A reason-illumined faith is important to him. "He is the best Christian," says Baxter, "who hath the readiest passage from the brain to the heart." Yet man can know no genuine growth unless he begins properly: "Christ is the door, the only way to this rest."

Following the appearance of Christ, the general resurrection and the last judgment (which will separate the saints from the sinners), those who take the proper "door" will discover what Baxter calls "the particular Excellencies of the Rest." One of the excellencies is that the rest is the proper and appropriate possession of the saints. Also cited as the motive for living a dedicated life is the enlargement of the spiritual capacities in order to become a proper and natural receptacle for the joys of heaven. In addition, the rest is excellent because it is a "seasonable" one. It is only after the vicissitudes of finite existence that heaven can be properly experienced. When the rest is received, it will be suitable to our perfected natures, our intensely divine desires and our corollary necessities. It will mean rest from all our doubts of God's love, because doubts will then be "weeded out" and will trouble the soul no more. Baxter says that there will be no such "language" as "How shall I know that God is my Father? Or, that my heart is upright? That my conversion is true? That faith is sincere?" All these questions will be turned into praise when the "excellencies" of rest are fully realized.

The excellencies of the saints stand out in bold relief as Baxter contrasts them with the state of those who will be denied everlasting rest. The unregenerate will have no part in the excellencies of the saints. They will know nothing of the fullness of God's love or of true fellowship with saints and angels. And the sense of their losses will be enhanced because then their understanding will be cleared and they will know the worth of what they have lost. "Understanding, conscience . . . memory must all live to torment them, which should have helped them to their happiness." And they will be tormented with the awareness that they sold their eternal welfare for the transitory delights of the flesh. Had they been forced to live in sin, it would "abate the rage of their consciences," but instead they have to exist with the haunting realization that they themselves willfully procured their own eternal destinies.

Baxter urges individuals to be certain beyond any shadow of doubt that they will not miss everlasting rest. And self-examination leads to certainty. Since it is possible for one to be deluded, Baxter suggests as guidelines to govern self-examination two significant questions: Is God the prime good of life? And do we accept Jesus Christ as our only Lord and Saviour? The first is the sum of the great command of the law, "Thou shalt love the Lord thy God with all thy heart," and the second is "the sum of the command" of the gospel, "Believe on the Lord Jesus Christ and thou shalt be saved."

The people of God, Baxter believes, have a special duty to "excite others" to seek this rest. The first step in exercising this duty is a spirit of compassion for men's souls. This should be followed by serious, zealous and effectual labor. Certain individuals are singled out by Baxter as having special responsibilities to help others. He refers particularly to those who possess knowledge and learning and those who have a gift for expressing thoughts effectively. But Baxter goes on to place responsibility on all who are acquainted with unregenerate men, and mentions specifically the opportunities of physicians and others in authority who can minister to men's spiritual needs. As for ministers, Baxter says, "it is the very work of their calling to help others to heaven."

Making clear that the saints' everlasting rest is unattainable on earth, Baxter believes man should spend much time contemplating the delights of the saints' rest. He should set his mind on heavenly matters. This will honor God, serve as a bulwark against temptation and aid the Christian in leading a godly life.

In stating directions on how to lead a "heavenly life upon earth," the author cautions against living in known sin, sharing the company of the ungodly, disputing over peripheral matters in Christian thought and possessing a proud and slothful spirit. Parallel to these instructions are positive suggestions for believers as guides for living the "heavenly life." Among these suggestions are the exhortations to engage in frequent conversations on the subject of eternal rest, to develop the habit of praising God, and to meditate on God's infinite love for the world. Meditation and prayer should occur frequently and at particular times and places.

The Lord's Day affords many opportunities for reflection on Christian matters, and regarding this, Baxter says: "Take notice of this, you that spend the Lord's Day only in public worship; your allowing no time to private duty, and therefore neglecting your spiritual duty of meditation, is very hurtful to your souls." Affliction, disappointment and bereavement should also be accepted as platforms on which God bestows new grace and strength for growth toward the "everlasting rest."

Leaving his reflections on how to live intensely a life of heavenly contemplation, Baxter closes his work with a moving prayer that he himself should not be a stranger to those joys which he describes to others.

Typical of much seventeenth century prose, Baxter's sentences are lengthy with subordinate clauses piled one on the other. But he also includes delightful statements that are terse and epigrammatic. Consider, for example, "Truth loseth more by loose friends than by sharpest enemies" or "Eternity is a piece of infiniteness."

Much of the persuasion in *Saints' Everlasting Rest* is built on the use of rhetorical questions. Also, in delineating his convictions, Baxter uses examples in the converse—noting what is likely to happen if the exhortation is *not* heeded: "Seldom conversing with Him will breed a strangeness betwixt thy soul and God."

The impact of the book is more than statements one can make on its content or its artistic structure. Baxter's creation emphasizes the sincerity, power and originality of a life and mentality focused on the conviction of Someone eternal behind the temporal appearance. This conviction and the Christian's response join forces in constructing a truer estimate of life, its source and its end.

JOHN BUNYAN (1628-1688)

John Bunyan was born the son of a tinker in the village of Elstow. He later served in the Puritan army. After reading a number of religious treatises circulating in the seventeenth century, Bunyan believed that he was predestined to everlasting damnation. He was almost driven to madness because of his deep anguish, but a Mr. Gifford of the Baptist Church at Bedford explained the Scriptures to Bunyan and showed him how he could have peace of soul in Christ. Following conversations with Mr. Gifford, which led to regeneration, Bunyan began to preach in small villages. His reputation grew, people in large numbers came to hear him preach and Bunyan was arrested and imprisoned under a Restoration Law which forbade such preaching missions. Once he was unable to speak face-to-face with the people, he began to channel his energies into writing. In prison he wrote his autobiography, *Grace Abounding to the Chief of Sinners.* In 1672, six years after the writing of the work, Bunyan was released from prison and became the pastor of a small church. Three years later he was again thrown into prison for six months. This time he began his masterpiece, *Pilgrim's Progress.* Though Bunyan is the author of many other religious works, *Grace Abounding* and *Pilgrim's Progress* deserve special attention.

GRACE ABOUNDING (1666)

This book belongs to a large class of spiritual autobiographies written by seventeenth century authors. Perhaps there is truth in the belief that because Puritans thought regeneration the central fact of human experience, they were particularly inclined to keep account of the minute details of their conversions. Whatever is the complete explanation for the writing of *Grace Abounding,* John Bunyan, the Puritan, graphically states the various pressures and patterns of thought and feeling through which he passed on his way to regeneration.

Although Bunyan tells very little about his boyhood, he does say that he descended from common people and his father's "rank was the meanest." But in spite of the poverty of his parents, Bunyan said, "It pleased God to put into their hearts to put me to school, to learn both to read and write."

Prior to his conversion, Bunyan believed there were few equal to him in the power to lie and curse. Because of the great displeasure which these habits brought to the Lord, Bunyan says that God scared and frightened him, even in his childhood, with "fearful dreams and dreadful visions." During these young years Bunyan was gripped by a great fear of the day of judgment. He was often so distressed that he wished there were no hell, or at least that he were a devil so that if he went to hell, he would be a tormentor rather than one tormented.

Soon, however, these fears left Bunyan, and losing himself in pleasure he became a ringleader of wayward youth. But in the midst of his wickedness Bunyan sometimes felt pangs of remorse;

and though he scorned the Christian religion, his heart trembled when he saw a Christian doing anything sinful.

After a term of military service with the Parliamentary army and following his marriage to a Christian woman, he began to think seriously on Christian matters. He read Christian books and attended church services, even taking part in some, but he still practiced many of his old habits.

Influenced by the minister's sermon, he began to ponder his violation of the Lord's Day. He went home from the services with a great burden, but soon the tugging convictions left him. One day, however, in the midst of a game of cat, he seemed to hear a voice from heaven bidding him to quit sinning or he would be sent to hell. Thinking anew of the state of his soul, he came to the conclusion that it was too late for him to know salvation. He so despaired of experiencing regeneration that he decided to take his fill of sin before he died.

Meanwhile Bunyan had stopped his habit of swearing. He had been reproached for his profanity by a woman shopkeeper, not particularly known for virtuous living, who told him that he was the most ungodly fellow she had ever heard in her life. Rebuke shamed Bunyan, and he declared that from the day of that reproof at least, he did not swear again. Following the incident he became acquainted with a poor Christian man who talked much about the Scriptures. Consequently Bunyan began to read the Bible for himself and used it as a "book of rules" for his life. His life was now outwardly different, and for about a year there seemed to be a marked change in his life. Yet he says that all of this time he was ignorant of Jesus Christ. Then one day in Bedford he heard some poor women, members of John Gifford's congregation, talking about the new birth and free grace and that "God had visited their souls with his love in the Lord Jesus." Talking with these women, he became greatly moved and sought out their pastor for consultation. His understanding of what it meant to experience the new birth deepened, but he continued to doubt and fear. Then one day he heard a minister preach: "Christ's love is without a cause; . . . Christ's love endures when hated of the world; and . . . Christ's love lasts, in spite of temptation, to the end." Bunyan now believed that his sins could be forgiven.

For a while Bunyan was literally exulting in the mercy and love of God, but before long questions and doubts again began to grip him. How could he be sure that the Scriptures were really the Word of God? How could he know that Jesus was really the Son of God? These were vexing and tormenting questions. "Everyone," Bunyan says, "doth think his own religion rightest, both Jews and Moors and Pagans! and how if all our faith, and Christ and Scriptures, should be but a think-so too?" The latter questions especially perplexed Bunyan, but his sense of God's presence in his life was too real for him to be troubled long by atheism and skepticism. Nevertheless the fear of possibly having committed the unpardonable sin still plagued him.

Finally this period of anguish gave way to Bunyan's assurance of salvation, for as he carefully studied the Scriptures he realized that as a believer in Christ he must claim the promises of God. Christ would not condemn any who placed their trust in Him. Bunyan then tells of his vision of the whole company of saints passing over into the New Jerusalem. Included in the record of this vision is a passage from the twelfth chapter of Hebrews which had at one time served as a focus for some of his most tormenting anxieties.

Bunyan became a member of the Rev. John Gifford's church and shortly thereafter began preaching in small villages. He had a special gift for preaching and within a short time hundreds were coming to hear him. After about five years of preaching, Bunyan tells of his arrest by the Crown in its drive for religious uniformity. Apparently he could have remained at liberty if he had agreed to stop preaching; but unwilling to stop, he had to go to prison.

Bunyan goes on to show that despite his preaching, he was never without fierce temptations and transitory fears. But his moments of temptations and fears always alternated with times of spiritual victories. In short, Bunyan's Christian life was a warfare.

Grace Abounding, a strong spiritual autobiography, uncovers a human experience in a simple, straightforward and unadorned manner. T. R. Glover's comment on *Grace Abounding* is pertinent: "Other men have had conflicts and reached the Celestial City, but few have had such a mastery of language, such a gift of seeing and hearing everything again as they write, such a force of sheer simplicity and truth."[13]

PILGRIM'S PROGRESS (Part I, 1678; Part II, 1684)

In the rhymed preface, an "Apology for his Book," Bunyan tells how his allegory *Pilgrim's Progress* came to be written. He says he was writing ". . . of the Way / and Race of Saints, in this our Gospel-day, / When he fell suddenly into an allegory." Even though the allegory formed itself in Bunyan's mind, he was apparently a bit suspicious of the creative imagination. Or he might have feared that some of his readers would think that an allegorical work lacked the solidity necessary in writings on divine matters. Responding to these fears, Bunyan writes:

> But must I needs want solidness, because
> By Metaphors I speak: Were not God's Laws,
> His Gospel-Laws, in olden times held forth
> By Types, Shadows, and Metaphors?

Bunyan showed his allegory to friends. Some advised him to publish it; others advised against it. Bunyan decided to have the work published in its allegorical form and was convinced he was justified in doing so. Commenting further on the form his work takes, Bunyan asserts, ". . . but yet let Truth be free / To make her sallies upon thee and me / Which way it pleases God." And further justifying his work, Bunyan contends:

> I find that Holy Writ in many places
> Hath semblance with this method, where the cases
> Do call for one thing, to set forth another;
> Use it I may then, and yet nothing smother
> Truth's golden Beams: nay, by this method may
> Make it cast forth its rays as light as day.

Bunyan's judgment was justified. No book with the exception of the Bible was to be so widely read for the next three centuries as *Pilgrim's Progress*, which has now been translated into practically every known language.

Pilgrim's Progress, Part I, relates the pilgrimage of Christian from the city of Destruction to the Celestial City. Aware of his sinful state, misunderstood by his family and scorned by his neighbors, he flees from his native place with a burden on his back and a book in his hand. Christian first meets Evangelist—a preacher of the Word—who tells him to head for the Wicket Gate. On his way to the Gate, Christian, accompanied by Pliable, gets bogged down in the Slough of Despond. At this point Pliable leaves Christian, but Help comes and shows him the steps that will take him out on the other side. Afterward Christian is way-laid by Mr. Worldly Wiseman who tries to turn him aside to the Town of Morality. Evangelist finds Christian, rebukes him, and again shows him the Wicket Gate. Entering through the Gate, Christian comes up a hill to the Cross, where his burden falls from his back. Three Shining Ones then clothe him with new raiment, place a mark on his forehead and give him a roll with a seal upon it. Christian is to look at the roll—his directions—as he continues his journey.

Coming from the Cross, Christian sees three men fast asleep with fetters upon their heels: Simple, Sloth and Presumption. Christian attempts to rouse them from their sleep. Simple replies, "I see no danger." As long as Simple's eyes are closed—by little-mindedness, by indifference, or for whatever reason—he does not suffer the shock of "fetters upon his heels." Sloth's response to Christian is, "Yet a little more sleep," and Presumption says, "Every Fat must stand upon his own bottom." Evading respon-sibility, Sloth and Simple procrastinate, living by little platitudes, and Presumption shows no indication of genuine concern for any-one, not even himself.

Christian journeys on and sees two men, Formalist and Hypoc-risy, trying to take a short cut to salvation. Confusing truth with custom, these two only laugh when Christian explains that there is a Door through which they must enter if they are to know sal-vation. After climbing the Hill Difficulty, Christian falls asleep and drops his roll, for which he has to return later.

Christian finds new joy at the House Beautiful in fellowship with the damsels Discretion, Prudence, Piety and Charity. He gains new strength here to meet his next hurdle—the fight with Apollyon in the Valley of Humiliation. Christian's encounter with Apollyon, who asks him to transfer his allegiance from God to Satan, comes after Christian has traveled a long way toward the Celestial City. Following this bout, Christian arrives at Vanity Fair, which lies directly across his path. Here Bunyan raises the question of the relation of Christian to the social order, and seems to show that man need not separate himself from the people of the social order, but from the vanities—the "fair" vanities—which unfit the Christian for a fine, spiritual life. Christian and Faithful (whom Christian meets prior to his entering Vanity Fair) call attention to themselves by their desire to buy nothing except truth at the fair. They are exposed in a cage, placed in prison, and finally brought to trial before Mr. Hategood, the judge, and before members of a jury which include Mr. Blindman, Mr. Malice, Mr. Love-lust, Mr. Live-loose, Mr. Hate-light and Mr. Implacable. Faithful is condemned to die and Christian is sent back to prison. Christian escapes from prison with Hopeful, "being made so," says Bunyan, "by the beholding of Christian and Faithful in their words and behavior, in their sufferings at the Fair."

Following the dramatic intensity of the trial scene and the escape of Christian, there follows a brief conversation between Christian and Mr. By-ends, who is from the town of Fair-speech. Mr. By-ends says he is bound for the Celestial City, but refuses to go in company with those who "must go against Wind and Tide" or with those who "must also own Religion in his Rags, as well as when in his Silver Slippers."

Crossing now a plain called Ease, Christian and Hopeful come to a Hill Lucre, and in that Hill is a Silver mine guarded by Demas. Because a Silver mine on a Hill is a rare sight, many turned aside to see it and perished as the "deceitful" ground broke under them. Christian and Hopeful do not heed the luring call of Demas, but By-ends and other companions who have now joined them become easy prey to him.

Christian and Hopeful move closer and closer to the Celestial City, and all seems to be going beautifully for them. They stop for a rest by the River of the Water of Life. But the way from the River is rough and the pilgrims want an easier way. Seeing a Stile that leads over to By-path meadow, they take the By-path route to Doubting Castle where they become prisoners of Giant Despair. There is no indication that the pilgrims deliberately chose the wrong route. They were simply deluded by By-path. After some wearisome experiences in Doubting Castle, Christian remembers that he possesses the Key of Promise that will unlock the door. Christian uses the key and soon they are on their journey again.

Most of the large hurdles are now passed. The journey's goal is in sight, but the pilgrim's life is a struggle to the very end. There is the final river to cross, and Bunyan says that Christian and Hopeful are "much astounded" at the river they, too, must cross. Passing through it, Christian begins to sink and almost drowns, but sustained and borne up by his companion, Hopeful, he at last enters the Celestial City.

Part II tells how Christian's wife, Christiana, undertakes the journey upon which she had refused to go with Christian. After Christian "crossed the River," she thought she had not only lost her husband but had hindered her sons "of Life." Repenting of her sins, she cries out to God for forgiveness. Christiana is called of God in the form of a letter from the King, smelling "after the manner of the best Perfume" and written "in letters of Gold," to make the same journey as her husband had taken.

Accompanied by Mercy, Christian's family starts the route to the Celestial City. Along the way they are joined by other pilgrims such as Mr. Greatheart (whom Roger Sharrock calls "the real successor to Christian in Part Two"), Mr. Honest, Mr. Valiant-for-truth, Mr. Steadfast, and Mrs. Much-afraid. The landmarks are much the same as those on Pilgrim's journey, but the burdens are not as heavy and the battles are not as great. "The atmosphere is more like that of a peace-time tour of the battlefields than of a new campaign."[14] At the Cross where the burden of Christian was "loosed from his back," Christiana and her company simply stop for reflection on the fact of Christ's death. They pass by Simple, Sloth and Presumption, "hanged up in irons, a little way off on the other side." The byways which Formalist and Hypocrisy took have since been "stopped up with chains, posts, and a ditch." The Hill Difficulty almost loses the significance of its name, for the hardest rigors are the "panting breaths" that it takes to climb in the "pelting heat." Outside the Palace Beautiful there is a giant, but he is soon subdued by Mr. Greatheart. Christiana and her family stay over a month in the House Beautiful, not primarily to receive new strength for the hard journey as in Christian's case, but for communal fellowship in spiritual matters. Vanity Fair is still held, but now a Christian community flourishes in the midst of Vanity.

Christiana's sons grow to manhood and assume their places of responsibility in the journey. Now Mr. Greatheart, with the new strength of the sons, draws up plans to attack Doubting Castle. He organizes an expedition, slays Giant Despair and liberates a number of prisoners held there. It is relevant to observe with Roland M. Frye that "all of Bunyan's giants represent man's pretension to more than human significance. . . . Their emphasis is on power, control, and dominion, apart from love."[15] Yet no giant, regardless of his pretended power, can prevent the Christian from reaching his destined goal.

The travelers come to the Delectable Mountains and, along with other pilgrims, await their respective calls to cross the river. When Christiana receives her call, Bunyan says: ". . . she came forth and entered the River, with a beckon of Farewell to those that followed her to the Riverside. The last word she was heard to say was, 'I come Lord, to be with thee and bless thee.' "

At Christiana's departure, her children weep, but Mr. Great-heart and Mr. Valiant play for joy upon the cymbal and the harp. As the various pilgrims hear their calls and cross the river of death, Bunyan describes the scene in one of his greatest prose passages of the entire book. He relates the final statements of the pilgrims as well as a glimpse of the other world: ". . . with Trumpeteers and Pipers, with Singers and Players on stringed Instruments, to welcome the Pilgrims as they went up, and followed one another in at the beautiful Gate of the City."

Regarding the style of *Pilgrim's Progress*, G. B. Harrison says: "Bunyan's style, except when he is deliberately quoting or imitating the Bible, is the best plain English. . . . He was not tempted to write the elaborate polysyllabic latinized English which passed for literary style among the learned."[16]

OTHER WORKS

Three of Bunyan's other works have been widely read: *The Life and Death of Mr. Badman*, the *Holy War* and *The Heavenly Footman*. *The Life and Death of Mr. Badman* (1680) is Bunyan's mirroring of the ungodly in his step-by-step journey from this world to hell. From birth to death, Mr. Badman is consistently evil without a trace of interest in good. As Bunyan depicts him on his journey, he is practically an evil puppet piling one evil deed upon another.

The *Holy War* (1682), Bunyan's longest work, uses the metaphor of the Christian life as conflict, and pictures the struggle between good and evil in man and in the world. The two forces rage in conflict under the figures of military combats, costly gains, retreats and at last, victory.

The Heavenly Footman (1698), another rather popular work, is a description of a man destined to go to heaven. Using the metaphor of life as a race, Bunyan describes the runner in his race for the heavenly prize. He makes clear that byways must be avoided, and the winner of the prize must go by the route of the cross.

That John Bunyan has a distinctive place in English literature is beyond question, and perhaps these words of Ola Winslow help one understand why:

> He is there because he looked deeply enough into himself to learn something about all men. He is there because he discovered one of the great themes which runs through human experience in all ages and then expressed it in simple words. He is there because he organized a segment of human experience in such a way as to give it shapeliness and meaning . . . . For many thousands of men and women through three centuries, Bunyan has taken religion out of the realm of confused mystery, made it personal, and given it a relation to life as it is lived in a practical world.[17]

JEREMY TAYLOR (1613-1667)

Jeremy Taylor, author, schoolmaster and preacher, was born in Cambridge. He received his early training at Perse school and later attended Gonville and Caius College, Cambridge. Taylor took orders in the Anglican Church in 1633, and shortly after this his eloquent preaching brought him to the attention of Archbishop Laud, who nominated him as a fellow at All Souls College, Oxford. A few months after Taylor became a fellow in the fall of 1636, Laud made him one of his own chaplains. Taylor also served as chaplain to the king and in the fall of 1638 was appointed "preacher to the University" at Oxford.

Taylor joined the Royalist forces during the Civil War and after his capture in the Royal defeat at Cardigan Castle (1645) he found refuge in Golden Grove, Carmarthenshire, where he wrote some of his best works. Later Taylor was taken prisoner on three different occasions. Following the Civil War, he spent most of his remaining life in Ireland.

Almost all of Jeremy Taylor's writings have a theological thrust. His *Liberty of Prophesying* (1647) is a strong plea for religious toleration and love toward people of varied beliefs. This work came at an opportune moment when strife and lack of charity were rampant amid the conflicts of religious opinion.

Of all Taylor's works the two which are still read are *The Rule and Exercises of Holy Living* and *The Rule and Exercise of Holy Dying*, both containing, as the titles suggest, spiritual directions for life and death. The latter was originally published separately, but the two works are often considered as one.

THE RULE AND EXERCISE OF HOLY LIVING AND HOLY DYING (1650-1651)

Taylor seems to be convinced that if one practices holy living he is prepared for death. At the same time if one is prepared for holy dying, he is also prepared to live a holy life. When Taylor speaks of holy living, he emphasizes the need for personal guidance from God in living a holy life.

In keeping with the characteristics of the literature of conduct (of which there was a great deal in the seventeenth century), Taylor covers the usual range of personal and social topics which need individual attention by any who would live a holy life.

Believing firmly that every man's profession or training should be looked upon as a calling from God and that one serves God in performing well his particular work, Taylor nevertheless insists that special deeds of devotion to God must be practiced if one is to live a holy life. He urges the individual to guard well his time, for "God hath given to man a short time here upon earth, and yet upon this short time eternity depends." Because so much is at stake in the way one cares for his time, Taylor urges that every possible moment be spent in prayer, meditation, charitable deeds and reading good books. Even the busiest person should set apart what he calls some "solemn time every year" or a period in which "quitting all worldly business, he may attend wholly to fasting and prayer, and the dressing of his soul by confessions, meditations and attendances upon God."

Along with Taylor's positive directions for holy living, he warns against any thoughts, attitudes or practices that would hinder the living of a holy life. Such things as "balls and revellings," "banquets and perfumes," and "garish and wanton dress," says Taylor, have a tendency to cause our affections to be focused on the world and should not be a part of a Christian's life. Taylor is particularly careful to caution against anything that would enhance pride.

If one is inclined even to think of his own humility, then there are ways of getting rid of false humility and of obtaining the true "grace of humility." Every day one should call to mind some one of his "foulest sins," or the "most shameful" of his disgraces, or his most indiscreet action. This should help allay any "present swelling of thy spirit," Taylor suggests.

Of particular interest is Taylor's view on obedience to superiors. Taylor's personal life definitely demonstrated his belief that subjects should obey the king. Consequently, it is not surprising that his writings contain the teaching of the absolute right of kings over subjects. Obedience to superiors, whether to parents or to the king, is a direct command of God. And rebellion or disobedience is one of the most impious acts of which man is capable. Moreover, it is a perversion of the very order of creation, and it is a sin committed in time which will condemn man for eternity.

As one would expect, Taylor spends much time on the inevitability of death. Yet holy living is a guaranteed preparation for holy dying. Because death is inevitable, man should avoid the futility of piling up riches or building a famous name for himself. Even long-range plans should not be made; for about the time one thinks his plans and dreams are about to be realized, he dies. The wise course is to "seize the day" or to use each moment with eternal matters in view and keep searching for the "abiding city" in the world to come.

Physical death should not be feared by the Christian believer if he has lived a holy life (Taylor has little or no respect for "death bed conversions," for he believes that an entire life should be lived for God). Even sickness, regardless of the misery it causes the Christian, should be considered as a friend and not an enemy, for illness and misery serve to turn one's affections from this world and enhance one's preparation for holy living and holy dying.

Jeremy Taylor has been called "the Shakespeare of English Prose." Perhaps the distinctive qualities of his literary powers are pinpointed in this tribute: "Taylor had that extraordinary gift of the visual imagination that enabled him to create not only a picture but a whole visual experience in a flashing comparison or sustained metaphor."[18]

JOHN MILTON (1608-1674)

Born in London of well-to-do and firmly Puritan parents, John

Milton studied first at St. Paul's and later at Christ's College, Cambridge. His enthusiasm for St. Paul's was most intense, but some of the bitterest diatribes in Milton's prose are leveled against his Cambridge experiences. Milton deeply appreciated the headmaster at St. Paul's and liked the critical training in the grammatical, logical and rhetorical analysis of Latin and Greek texts as well as training in the art of writing and discoursing in those languages. Cambridge was still a stronghold of Scholasticism, and there Milton found himself examining the classical texts in order to engage in scholastic debates on purely formal subjects, presumably with a view to acquiring training in logic. But Milton rebelled against this approach to education. He once referred to these teachers of logic as those who "taught people to be accurate simpletons." At Cambridge, nevertheless, he decided that someday he would become a great poet and write poetry of such caliber as "posterity should not willingly let die." Being a poet was a high calling to John Milton; a poet was priest and prophet, and he must be well prepared to fulfill his lofty responsibility.

In 1632 Milton took his Master of Arts degree and then went to live at his father's house in the village of Horton a short distance from London. He continued his studies independently at Horton from 1632 to 1638. During these six years he read widely in the literature of Rome, Greece, Italy, France, Spain and England, and also became thoroughly familiar with the Bible, the Talmud and the writings of the early Church Fathers.

The first period of Milton's writing was almost exclusively dedicated to poetry. His literary output at the beginning of the Horton period was not particularly impressive, for he had at that time written only such works as his *Academic Prolusions*, a few sonnets and an ode. But Milton himself in his sonnet "On His Being Arrived to the Age of Twenty-three" (1631) suggested a discouragement that he had as yet accomplished little of quality:

> How soon hath Time, the subtle thief of youth,
> Stolen on his wing my three and twentieth year!
> My hasting days fly on with full career,
> But my late spring no blood or blossom show'th.

But toward the end of those years at Horton it was evident that John Milton was a poet—he had written "Comus" and "Lycidas" as well as his companion pieces "L'Allegro" and "Il Penseroso."

The second period of Milton's career (1641-1654) is primarily one of prose writing. He knew he must write a great poem, but was willing to postpone his own poetic ambitions in order to enter the field of polemic prose and use his talents primarily on one subject—liberty. This is the period of his argumentative prose on church government when he attacked the Episcopal form of church government and pleaded for the Presbyterian. Convinced that the Presbyterian form guarantees more individual freedom, Milton struck hard at the lack of democracy in the structure of the Episcopacy and the overlordliness of the Anglican hierarchy of his time.

Five anti-Episcopal pamphlets were written during the years of 1641-1642. In 1643-1645 Milton wrote four tracts on divorce which provoked bitter criticism for his broad, revolutionary ideas. What Milton held was generally in opposition to the views on marriage and divorce of Catholics and various other religious groups. Convinced that marriage was not a sacrament which only the church could dissolve, Milton contended that it was a contract entered into by two people, which might be voided for sufficient cause, and to Milton incompatibility—particularly intellectual incompatibility—was a sufficient cause for divorce. In fact, to Milton incompatibility was a better argument for divorce than adultery.

Milton's next important prose works were *Of Education* (1644), and *Areopagitica,* perhaps his most important treatise, published the same year. After three centuries many of his educational principles expounded in *Of Education* are still timely and relevant. Running throughout the treatise is the clear indication that excellence in education requires discipline and tenacity of purpose. Milton urges the supplementing of books with personal or practical experience, but this view must always be kept within the context of the high scholarly purpose of his educational standards.

The *Areopagitica* is frequently referred to as the greatest classical oration in the English language. His primary plea is for freedom of the press and for freedom of the individual to read wherever his inquiring mind leads him. But John Milton draws a sharp line between liberty and license. License is irresponsible liberty which Milton could not tolerate.

Writing his oration in the form of a speech addressed to Parliament, Milton makes use of all the arts of rhetoric to convince and persuade his readers of the need for unlicensed printing. Incensed by the new licensing law of June, 1643, Milton attempted to show that the act would fail to ban the books at which it was directed and could hamper the search for truth. Again and again he returns to the argument that an act of Parliament cannot make people virtuous since virtue depends on the freedom of the individual to choose.

Milton's next group of prose pamphlets was on political liberty, several of which were written between 1649 and 1660. And it should be remembered that by 1652 Milton was blind. His writing was still for the most part in prose, and his great poetic work which he believed he must write was not yet written. His prose works of this period include a *History of Britain* and *Of Christian Doctrine*. The latter work contains Milton's position on the basic doctrines of the Christian faith, and his view of Christ in particular—that God the Son is inferior in essence to God the Father.

In 1656 Milton married Katherine Woodcock, his former wife, Mary Powell, having died in 1652. Katherine Woodcock died in 1658 with the daughter to which she had given birth.

The third period and the greatest of Milton's writings began in 1655 and lasted until a few years before his death. Included in this period are *Paradise Lost, Paradise Regained, Samson Agonistes* and the sonnets. Milton married again in 1663 and his wife, thirty years younger, was a most devoted companion.

Choosing the "religious literature" from among Milton's many works is not an easy task. Consideration is given to selected works.

SELECTED SHORT POEMS

"Ode on the Morning of Christ's Nativity" (1629)

The poem begins with a four-stanza introduction and is followed by the main part of the work called "The Hymn." In the introduction Milton announces the theme and his occasion for writing the poem. It is the birthday of the Christ Child, and Milton presents his poem as a gift to the newly born Christ. The Wise Men from the East are bringing their gifts, and Milton will go before them bringing his ode as a gift.

The hymn follows with a more complete and artistic description of what Milton announces in the introductory stanzas. In the first half of the hymn there is a world of stillness, peace and music. But Milton says: ". . . wisest Fate says NO, / This must not yet be so." So, in sharp contrast to the first half of the hymn, the second half is a world of darkness, noise and weeping. Temporarily there was a peace on earth when the Christ Child came, but the Babe must grow up and be crucified on the cross before man knows salvation. When He completes His final work, the heroic Christ will have destroyed all pagan deities and the power of evil will continue no longer in the world.

Sonnet XIX, "When I Consider . . ." (1655)

Milton develops the sonnet on his blindness around the metaphor in the parable of the talents (Matthew 25:14-30). "That one Talent which is death to hide" moves Milton to ask restlessly whether God expects him to continue his labors even though he is blind: "Doth God exact day-labor, light denied." The questioning ceases with a recognition of and a resignation to the conviction, "They also serve who only stand and wait."

PARADISE LOST (1665)

Paradise Lost is an epic poem literally packed with treasures of learning. The Hebraic and Hellenic streams of culture are built into the poem in such a manner that extensive learning is obviously in the very tissue of Milton's thinking. For years Milton pondered possibilities for the subject of the poem that he knew he must write, and for a time he considered writing on the Arthurian legend. Finally he chose the subject of the fall of Adam and Eve.

Book I

Following the example of classical epics, Milton states immediately his subject—man's first disobedience. The reference is to *man,* not to Satan. Notice, too, that mention is made early of "one greater Man" who will restore disobedient man.

As one reads the first prologue, which consists of twenty-six lines, he finds that Milton is writing an epic, based on classical models, but with the aid of the "Heavenly Muse" (an invocation to a muse is also an epic characteristic). Milton hopes to transcend the classical with a loftier theme and then "to justify the ways of God to man."

In epic fashion the story proper begins *in medias res*, showing Satan and his cohorts, the rebel angels, lying stupefied on a burning lake of Hell where they have been thrown after their defeat in Heaven. Recovering a bit from his stupor, Satan encourages Beelzebub and tells him that they could yet wage successful war, by force or guile, against the One who had overpowered them. Satan then tries to comfort all his troops with the possibility of their regaining Heaven, and commands them to form a council in order to decide upon the next course of action. The fallen angels build Pandemonium, the palace of Satan, and in it the leaders of these rebels sit in council.

Book II

The council in Hell begins. Satan, the "chairman" of the council, opens the debate on whether they should attempt another war against Heaven. One gets to know the fallen angels quite intimately as they show their thinking on the subject for debate. Moloch, the first to speak, Milton introduces as "the strongest and the fiercest spirit / That fought in Heaven; now fiercer by despair." He gives his position in the first six words, "My sentence is for open war." Belial, the next speaker, is the antithesis of Moloch. Suave, oratorical, "graceful and humane," Belial makes a long, subtle speech that confuses the real issues, but it finally comes through that he is against war.

As one breaks through Belial's hairsplitting quibbles, he discovers that Belial has shredded Moloch's proposal. Belial warns that it would not be a simple process to get back to Heaven, for angels are on guard all around. And even if they could force themselves back, there is the possibility of total annihilation, and Hell is certainly preferable to annihilation. So Belial urges that they remain where they are. Maybe, too, there will be a repeal of their punishment.

Mammon, the next speaker, does not want war and does not want to go back to Heaven. To him it would be a "wearisome Eternity" if he had to spend it singing "forced hallelujahs" to the One who cast him out of Heaven in the first place. So he urges that they forget about Heaven and in his words: "Live to ourselves, though in this vast recess, / Free, and to none accountable, preferring / Hard liberty before the easy yoke / Of servile pomp."

But the real nature of Mammon's perspective becomes clear when he says, "This desert soil / Wants not her hidden luster, gems and gold; / Nor want we skill or art, from whence to raise / Magnificence; and what can Heaven show more?"

Mammon's position is unmistakable: the fallen angels are creative, and their new world contains an abundance of natural resources, so they merely need to go to work and build a new, good world for and from themselves. Since Heaven is undoubtedly just a material place to Mammon, he would simply build up Hell and make it another magnificent, material place and a rival kingdom to Heaven.

Mammon's proposal receives enthusiastic reception from the fallen angels, and this must have perturbed Satan, for it is obvious from the very beginning of the pseudodemocratic meeting that Satan has his own proposal and expects it to be followed.

Satan's spokesman, Beelzebub, the next speaker, shows in the first part of his discourse the unrealistic nature of the first three speeches. Beelzebub tells the fallen angels of a more practicable way of revenge. In place of the third part of angels who fell, their "Conqueror," informs Beelzebub, intends to create another world, "the happy seat / Of some new race call'd Man." The new race is to love and serve Him and in time will replace the angels who rebelled. Beelzebub proposes that the best way to get revenge against God will be to find this new world and either drive out the new inhabitants, or even better, "Seduce them to our party, that their God / May prove their Foe, and with repenting hand / Abolish his own works." Beelzebub's next move is to show how perilous the uncharted journey is to man's world. And the big question becomes: Who is courageous enough to go? As he planned from the beginning, Satan volunteered to carry out the mission. Setting forth on the hazardous journey, Satan comes first to the gate of Hell which is guarded by Sin and Death. After bargaining with these two ugly creatures, Satan persuades them to open the gates for him and proceeds on his way.

Some readers of Milton's *Paradise Lost,* and particularly readers of only the first two books, get overly impressed with Satan and want to make him the hero of Milton's epic. No one would question the greatness with which Satan is depicted. Milton is too fine an artist not to do justice to his villain. However, careful notice must be given to the exact manner in which Milton draws the greatness of Satan: The greatness lies not primarily in the flamboyant heroism characteristic of Books One and Two, but in the slow deterioration of an angel who once stood next to God in Heaven to a monstrous serpent who, surrounded by his ugly, fallen cohorts, lay "on his belly chewing ashes." Through the gradual diminishing of Satan from grandeur to baseness, Milton with artistic subtlety brings the reader from sleazy admiration to discerning comprehension of the fallen angel's nature.

Book III

Opening with a beautiful "Prologue to Light," Book Three shows God on His throne in Heaven. Seeing Satan on his way to man's world, God the Father points him out to God the Son and foretells Satan's deception of mankind. God explains that though man has been created able to stand, yet man will fall.

Christ offers Himself as a ransom for fallen man, and God accepts His offer and tells of the coming incarnation. Following the Son's offer to become man and suffer man's punishment, there are scenes of great exaltation and celebration. Milton says of the angelic hosts, "Lowly reverent / Towards either throne they bow, and to the ground / With solemn adoration down they cast / Their crowns."

Meanwhile Satan continues his journey and Milton pictures him as "ready now / To stoop with wearied wings and willing feet / On the bare outside of this World." After waiting on the "bare outside" of this world, Satan moves on until he comes to the orb of the Sun where he sees an angel whom he recognizes to be Uriel, "one of the seven / Who in God's presence, nearest to His throne, / Stands ready to command." Changing himself into a "stripling Cherub," Satan talks with Uriel and pretends that he has come to see the new creation and man. Deceived by Satan, Uriel points out the particular orb which contains the dwelling place of man. Ironical it is that Uriel, one of God's servants, gives Satan the desired directions which enable him to go hastily to man's world on his fatal mission. The disguising of Satan in order to hide his identification and his motivation causes Milton to stop and interject a perceptive thought on hypocrisy — "For neither man nor Angel can discern Hypocrisy—the only evil that walks / Invisible, except to God alone."

Book IV

Satan is in view of Eden as the book opens. Before Milton describes the garden, he gives further insight into the character of Satan. Through the literary device of the soliloquy, in which a character speaks honestly and frankly about himself, Milton gives another view of the real Satan. "Inflamed with rage," and falling into many doubts with himself, Satan shows marks of uncertainty about the success of his mission. And as he talks with himself, he admits that it was not God's fault that he was hurled from Heaven; he knows the fault lies with himself. He acknowledges that repentance is possible, but it would involve submission and he says, "and that word / Disdain forbids me, and my dread of shame / Among the Spirits beneath, whom I seduc'd / With other promises and other vaunts / Than to submit." Pride is still there. Power of free will is also at work, for now Satan, deliberately choosing not to repent or submit, continues to hold to his maxim, "Evil, be thou my good." The soliloquy helps to modulate Satan down from the grand figure of Books One and Two. Changes in his physical appearance also reflect his moral degeneration: "His face, / Thrice changed with pale—ire, envy, and despair." But the "Artificer of Fraud" moved on like "a prowling wolf" attacking sheep or like "a thief bent to unhoard the cash / Of some rich Burgher." He then comes in closer for a view of the Garden of Eden and of those who dwell there.

The Garden of Eden and Adam and Eve are beautifully described. Satan marvels at all the beauty he beholds. He delivers a tortured speech upon seeing the happy relation between Adam and Eve and yet delights in the prospect of their destruction through his cunningness. He overhears a conversation between Adam and Eve in which they speak of the fruit of the Tree of Knowledge of Good and Evil, that one tree of which they must not eat. In that "one easie prohibition," Satan will do his destructive work.

Meanwhile the angel Uriel comes to the gate of Paradise which is guarded by the angel Gabriel. Uriel warns Gabriel that, under the guise of a good angel, an evil one had slipped by him. Gabriel says he will find the evil one before morning. Milton then gives a picture of Adam and Eve in the evening as they discuss their labors of the day, as they worship God and as they retire for the night. As the lovers sleep, Satan begins his ugly work by whispering in Eve's ear through a dream. Gabriel's angels, specifically summoned to guard Paradise, find Satan, "Squat like a toad" at Eve's ear. The book ends on a note of ominous foreboding.

Book V

Opening with a lovely description of dawn in Paradise and the awaking of Adam and Eve, Book Five reveals the nature of the dream that Satan put into Eve's mind. It was a "prophetic dream," outlining in detail the actual temptation. Eve is disturbed and tells of "this uncouth dream." Briefly applying the "faculty psychology" of Milton's day, Adam explains to Eve that the human personality consists of reason, fancy and imagination, and on the hierarchical scale, reason is chief. While one sleeps, Adam continues, "Mimic Fancy" imitates reason, and in dreams one makes irrational combinations because reason is not in ascendance. Since Eve's dream seems to come from the fancy and because she did not give her approval to the suggestion of the dream, then she should not be disturbed. Eve is comforted by Adam's explanation, but she is not completely satisfied, for Milton says, "and she was cheered / But silently a gentle tear let fall / From either eye." And this is Milton's first account of human tears falling in Paradise.

Before Adam and Eve begin their work of tending the plants, they offer "unmeditated" prayers and praise to God. On this day they have an angelic visitor. God, knowing the origin of Eve's perturbing dream, sends Raphael to give man all the knowledge he needs to resist Satan. The preparation of the two to entertain their first guest is one of the most charming in the epic. Adam meets Raphael "without more train / Accompanied than with his own complete / Perfections . . . Yet . . . bowing low." Eve is described in her innocent beauty, "Eve, / Undeckt, save with herself, more lovely fair . . . Stood to entertain her guest from Heaven. . . ." Raphael, going into great detail about the hierarchical order, warns Adam of his great enemy, Satan. Listening respectfully to Raphael, Adam then requests more information on the history of Satan. Raphael gives an account of Satan's move to incite a third of the angels in Heaven to rebel against God.

The description of the warfare in Heaven is actually the beginning of the story, for in epic fashion Milton started *in medias res.*

Book VI

The entire book is largely Raphael's narration. Michael and Gabriel are sent to battle against Satan and his rebel angels. Following the first fight, Satan and his followers are forced to withdraw. They sit in council and decide on new instruments of destruction which cause much confusion in Michael's ranks in the second day's fight. However, by tearing up the mountains—with their piles of rocks, wood and water—and throwing them at their enemies, the loyal angels overpower Satan and his cohorts. On the third day God sent His Son to stop the rebellion. "The Chariot of Paternal Deity" moves with mighty force against the enemy. The Son pursues them to the wall of Heaven and down the rebels fall "from the verge of Heav'n; eternal wrath / Burnt after them to the bottomless pit."

Book VII

Along with the preceding book, the seventh book has received considerable criticism for its lack of poetic originality. Continuing the narration of how the new universe was created by God, Milton does largely follow the Genesis record, but it is obvious that his own imagination adds many details as he describes the account of each day's creative work.

With the creation of man on the sixth day, the creative work reaches its climax. One of the most arresting impressions of the entire book is the pervasive sense of happiness throughout creation prior to and at the time of the creation of man. Something of this glad spirit prior to creation is captured in these lines: "Now Heaven in all her glory shone, and rolled / Her motions, as the great First Mover's hand / First wheeled their course; Earth in her rich attire / Consummate, lovely smiled; air, water, earth / By fowl, fish, beast, was flown, was swum, was walked." Then, as Adam is formed into life, he hears the music of all creation: "the sound / Symphonious of ten thousand harps, that tuned / Angelic harmonies. The earth, the air / Resounded (thou remember'st, for thou heard'st); The Heavens and all the constellations rung, / The planets in their stations listening stood, / While the bright pomp ascended jubilant."

Book VIII

With the angel's comments on the motions of the heavenly bodies, Raphael's narration concludes. At Raphael's request Adam gives an account of his first days on earth. One of the most engaging parts of Adam's discourse is the account of his conversation with God on the subject of a mate. Adam tells God that there is not much fun in solitude. God replies that Adam is not solitary and asks Adam, "Is not the Earth / With various living creatures, and the Aire, / Replenisht, and all these at thy command / To come and play before thee?" To this Adam argues that the animals are not his equal and "Among unequals . . . what harmonie or true delight?" God then, as though He were teasing Adam, tells him that He is ". . . alone / From all Eternitie." But Adam tells God that He is perfect and does not need a mate. After a few more comments from Adam, the conversation concludes with God informing Adam that He intended from the beginning to give him a mate.

Adam then tells of the creation of Eve and of his own excitement over her loveliness and power. Adam says, "yet when I approach / Her loveliness, so absolute she seems / And in herself complete, so well to know / Her own, that what she wills to do or say / Seems wisest, virtuousest, discreetest, best." And so Adam's adulation continues, and Raphael breaks in and warns him of allowing his passion to overcome his reason. At the close of the book, Raphael repeats the warning: ". . . take heed lest Passion sway / Thy judgment to do aught, which else free Will / Would not admit." Following an elaboration of the repeated warning, Raphael departs and Adam is now on his own—sufficient to stand, but free to fall.

Book IX

After Milton gives a defense of his Christian epic in a brief prologue, he turns his attention to Satan, about whom he has said nothing since Book Four, except for the account of the warfare in Heaven. Making clear again the degeneration of Satan, Milton pictures him as "a black mist low-creeping." He finds the serpent sleeping, and "In at his mouth / The Devil entered."

Coming nearer to the crisis of the poem, Milton shows Adam and Eve discussing the latter's suggestion that they work in different parts of the garden. She wants to prove her own virtue, and uses almost the same argument about "untried virtue" that Milton uses in the *Areopagitica* and also in "Comus." Adam reluctantly consents to Eve's working alone and reasons, "thy stay, not free, absents thee more." David Daiches says, "as Eve slides her hand out of her husband's, Milton uses the richest resources of classical mythology to dwell for the last time on her innocence and beauty."[19] Milton does seem to tarry on his comparisons of Eve with the innocent and beautiful of classical times in order to impress indelibly upon the reader exactly what the unfallen Eve is like. She is undoubtedly never lovelier than at this parting scene, and the Eve who returns makes the contrast between what she *was* and what she *is* inescapable and emotionally wearing.

Eve's temptation and fall are complex and demand a close scrutiny of the Tempter as well as of the nature of the temptation. The serpent finds Eve alone. He comes before her in great splendor, not prone on the ground, but rising in towering folds; with "burnisht neck of verdant gold" and eyes like "carbuncles," "Pleasing was his shape, / And lovely; never since of Serpent kind / Lovelier." In addition to the serpent's staggering splendor, he can also speak, and says that he has attained the power of speech and reason by eating of a particular fruit in the garden.

The first device in Satan's temptation of Eve is flattery. He tells her that all living things adore her beauty and look at her "with ravishment" from afar. Trying to persuade Eve that her beauty deserves universal admiration, he urges her not to waste it upon beasts and the one man who is with her in the garden. Eve hears the serpent, of course, but she seems to marvel more at his gift of speech than at the probability of her being such a ravishing beauty.

The next tool used by Satan is hypocrisy, and Milton has already said that "neither man nor angel can discern / Hypocrisie— the only evil that walks / Invisible, except to God alone." Assuring Eve that his transformation into a talking, reasoning beast came from eating the fruit from a particular tree, Satan arouses Eve's curiosity and interest in seeing this unusual tree. He leads her to the tree, which she recognizes as the Tree of the Knowledge of Good and Evil. Her immediate reaction is that God said, "Ye shall not eat thereof, nor shall ye touch it, lest ye die."

Satan now moves into the third stage of the temptation and uses the device of argument. His speech is "crammed with specious arguments with sequences that look like syllogisms but stop before they have arrived . . . that sound as if they are reaching a conclusion but do not quite reach it, and the ground is shifted every few seconds."[20] Satan tries to show that the tree gives life to knowledge and she will surely not die from eating its fruit. After all, God did not punish the serpent for eating it, and it would surely be absurd to punish mankind. God has threatened death simply to test her courage, Satan rationalizes; and besides, God would be unjust if He punished her for "such a petty trespass." And certainly if He is unjust, He cannot be God. God is simply jealous and does not want man to become godlike. The logic sounds appealing and convincing to Eve, but what she does not know is who the serpent is and that the pseudoargument is based on a lie.

A serpent of staggering splendor uses flattery, then hypocrisy, and finally, specious argumentation. But Eve has not yet fallen. One more factor must be considered. It is noon. Eve is hungry and thirsty, and her mind is confused. She begins to ponder what the serpent has said and, after musing for a while, she even adds another faulty argument: God named the Tree of Knowledge and apparently has forbidden man to be wise. So, "What hinders then to reach and feed at once both body and mind." Following this question, Milton immediately describes the next move this way: "So saying, her rash hand in evil hour / Forth reaching to the Fruit, she pluck'd, she eat." Eve eats to excess. She even speaks of going on a steady diet of the luscious fruit until she grows "mature / In knowledge, as the Gods who all things know." At first she thinks she will keep this knowledge even from Adam, but then decides that it just might be true as God said, that if you eat of the fruit you shall die. Then, too, if she dies and leaves Adam, he would marry another Eve and be happy with her. So she comes to Adam with the fruit. Adam is waiting for her with a garland of roses, but upon seeing Eve "From his slack hand the garland wreathed for Eve / Down dropped, and all the faded roses shed." What a contrast between the Eve that returns to Adam and the Eve who left him! In a kind of drunken lilt she talks to Adam of her experiences. Adam is astonished, and he does not reproach her (the reproaches come later), but what he intends to do about the fruit is obvious: "I feel / The link of Nature draw me: flesh of Flesh, / Bone of my bone thou art, and from thy state / Mine never shall be parted, bliss or woe."

Permitting passion to triumph over reason, and disregarding his place in the hierarchical order, Adam deliberately eats of the forbidden fruit, and immediately a change is wrought in him. Parodying God's speech to him regarding a companion, Adam now addresses Eve in nasty, sarcastic words.

In summarizing the changes in the relation between Adam and Eve immediately after the fall, David Daiches says, "Sex becomes guilty now; images suggesting drunkenness and irresponsibility are rife in Milton's account of the first postlapsarian sexual act, and they awake from the restless sleep that follows with the new knowledge of shame. A new kind of self-consciousness is present, and it destroys all their satisfaction in their mutual relationship. . . . The pair bickers with sullen regret and mutual reproachfulness . . . ."[21] Adam and Eve disobeyed God; they defied the hierarchical plan for man and the universe, and Book Nine ends in empty despair.

Book X

The action begins in Heaven when the "heinous" act becomes known to an omniscient God. The angelic guard is sad, but God exonerates them from blame, telling them that man had free will to stand or to fall, and he chose to fall.

God sends the Son to judge and to pass sentence on Adam and Eve. Woman shall in pain and travail bring forth children. Man shall learn that the ground is cursed and in sorrow he shall eat of it, for God said, "in the sweat of thy face shalt thou eat bread."

Aware of Satan's victory, Sin and Death decide to go to man's world. There they meet Satan, who lurks suspiciously about Eden by night in order to determine the results of his temptation. Sin and Death stay in the new world to spread their evil influence, but Satan returns to Hell where he tells of his successful venture. Expecting great applause from his audience, he stands proudly before them to receive their adulation. But instead "he hears / On all sides from innumerable tongues, / A dismal univeral hiss, the sound / Of public scorn." And Satan, who once stood next to

God in Heaven, becomes a serpent, "punished in the shape he sinned."

Meanwhile Eve begins the process of reconciliation with Adam, but it is a slow beginning. Though Eve approaches him with "soft words," Adam storms at her with the stern reply, "Out of my sight, thou serpent!" Forgetting that he had asked God for a companion, he now cries out, "Oh, why did God, / Creator wise, that peopl'd highest Heaven / With spirits Masculine, create at last / This novelty on Earth, this fair defect / Of Nature . . .?" In tears Eve falls at Adam's feet, acknowledges her wrong, and wishes that she may be permitted to bear the punishment for both. Soon Adam's heart relents, and at the close of Book Ten Milton says of Adam and Eve: "And both confessed / Humbly their faults, and pardon begg'd, with tears / Watering the ground. . . ."

Book XI

The Son of God presents the prayers of the repentant Adam and Eve to God the Father. The Father accepts the intercession of the Son, but declares that Adam and Eve must leave the Garden of Eden. The angel Michael is sent down to banish the pair. When the angel tells the two why he has come, they are both struck with sorrow. Having "drencht" Eve's eyes with sleep, Michael leads Adam to the top of a high hill in Paradise where they look out upon a series of events in the history of Adam's offspring up to the flood.

Book XII

Michael's vision of events continues. Events after the flood to the incarnation, death, resurrection and ascension of Christ as well as the history of man to the second advent of Christ are unfolded. Having received extensive teaching concerning the future, Adam responds to the angel with significant words:

> Greatly instructed I shall hence depart,
> Greatly in peace of thought, and have my fill
> Of knowledge, what this vessel can contain;
> Beyond which was my folly to aspire.
> Henceforth I learn, that to obey is best,
> And love with fear the only God. . . .

Descending the hill with Adam, Michael tells him to share what he has learned with Eve and particularly of "the great deliverance by her seed to come . . . on all mankind."

Obeying the command of God, Michael leads Adam and Eve from the garden. Milton closes his great literary epic with attention focused upon them as they leave the Garden of Eden:

> Some natural tears they dropp'd, but wip'd them soon;
> The World was all before them, where they chose
> Their place of rest, and Providence their guide
> They hand in hand with wand'ring steps and slow,
> Through Eden took their solitary way.

These last few lines end the epic, but it is fitting that John Milton gave the last spoken words of this tragedy of man's disobedience not to Adam but to Eve, the first to sin and the first to repent. Her words are pregnant with significance: "though all by me is lost . . . / By me the Promised Seed shall all restore."

PARADISE REGAINED (1671)

Paradise Regained is a short epic which presents a vivid study of Christ as an epic hero. Sometimes referred to as a philosophic dialogue on ends and means, *Paradise Regained* shows the means which Satan uses in order to attempt to hinder Christ from attaining His declared end.

The four books deal with Satan's temptation of Christ and the power of Christ to stand against His tempter. Milton uses as his chief source material the gospel story as it is given in Luke chapter 4. Expanding the Luke account into two thousand lines, Milton spends most of his energy on the second temptation, for in spite of the expansion he dismisses the first and third temptations in fifty lines.

Some influence of Spenser's *Faerie Queene* is discernible in *Paradise Regained*, and there is perhaps a slight use of Giles Fletcher's poem "Christ's Victory and Triumph." (Fletcher is another seventeenth century poet who wrote on the temptation of Christ. He is sometimes referred to as a link between Spenser and Milton, but his artistic power does not begin to equal either of the other two poets.) For the structure of Milton's short epic, he was probably influenced by the book of Job, particularly in using passages primarily of dialogue with short connecting narrative sections. But *Paradise Regained,* as *Paradise Lost,* is filled with Milton's own extensive knowledge of Hebraic and Hellenic culture which he shapes and molds for his own artistic purposes.

Book I

Christ, after His baptism in Jordan, is led into the wilderness. In a brief scene in Heaven, God informs Gabriel that He is deliberately exposing Christ to Satan's wiles. God says of Satan, "He now shall know I can produce a man / Of female Seed, far abler to resist / All his solicitations, and at length / All his vast force, and drive him back to Hell." Satan will learn that God cannot and will not be conquered by him.

Remaining in the wilderness forty days and nights, Christ grows hungry, for during this time He has not tasted "human food." Satan approaches Christ in His hunger and urges Him to command that the stones be made bread. The Son of God knows who the tempter is and tells him that man does not live by bread alone. Then He questions, "Why dost thou then suggest to me distrust / Knowing who I am, as I know who thou art?" Replying in smooth and hypocritical words, Satan insists that he is still the servant of God, and, although he has lost God's love, he has not lost his ability to love, or at least to admire, good and virtue in others. Finding that his smooth talk makes no impact upon Christ, Satan disappears "into thin air diffused."

Book II

The scene shifts for a time back to Galilee and gives a glimpse of the disciples, as well as Christ's mother, becoming concerned over the absence of Christ. Satan returns to his cohorts to report that he has had no success so far in his temptation of Christ. But Satan departs to continue further strategy, taking with him a "chosen band of spirits likest to himself in guile."

The scene now returns to the wilderness where concentration on the second temptation begins. Jesus is sleeping and dreams of Elijah, who was fed by ravens and an angel, and of Daniel, who refused to eat the meat offered by Nebuchadnezzar. Prior to the dream, Jesus speaks of feeling pangs of hunger. Soon after the dream, Satan appears and brings before the Christ a magnificent banquet, described in words of beauty and splendor reminiscent of the language of *Paradise Lost*. Again Jesus proves that He can withstand the temptation even though He is hungry and can see and smell the lavish feast. Satan has failed in his attempt to make Christ settle for bodily satisfaction by appealing to His judgment through the appetite.

Changing the nature of his appeal, Satan tells Christ that since "all thy heart is set on high designs," he must know means of reaching his high goals which to Satan are riches, wealth and treasure. And if Christ "hearkens" to Satan, he will bestow these prerequisites—according to the tempter, the sole prerequisites—to greatness. Jesus replies emphatically to Satan that wealth without virtue, valor and wisdom is impotent "to gain dominion or to keep it gained."

Book III

Further tempting Christ to attain honor and glory through wrong means, Satan brings before Him a catalog of prominent historical figures, all of whom had become famous before they were as old as Jesus. He reviews the accomplishments of Alexander the Great, Scipio and Pompey, and then adds the name of Julius Caesar "Whom now all the world admires," but who "wept that he had liv'd so long inglorious." Following a discourse in which Christ explains the essence of true glory, He then points out Job as one who might not have been well known on earth, "where glory is false glory," but was famous in Heaven. Job exemplified the true virtues of patience and temperance. This emphasis upon moral virtues seems to be picked up by Satan, who asks Christ if the deliverance of Israel from the Roman yoke would not be a good thing. Why not fight a good, righteous war against the heathen? But Jesus replies with a straightforward statement, "All things are best fulfilled in due time." Satan presses his point, takes Christ up on a high mountain, and urges Him to accept his help in regaining David's throne. Pointing out the Parthian Army, indicative of strength, efficiency and power, Satan tells Christ that when He ascends David's throne this military might will insure safety and will mean a sure deliverance of the ten tribes. In line with His previous response Jesus says the people of Israel will be brought back in God's own time. Besides, He does not need military means in order to ascend the throne.

Book IV

Satan is perplexed as the book opens. His sleek tongue had worked so well on Eve, "but *Eve* was *Eve* / This far his overmatch."

Continuing the second temptation of earthly glory, Satan now tempts with political fame and shows Christ a glorious picture of the color, movement and variety of the whole Roman world. The extent and grandeur of the capital of the world at that time are imaginatively presented. And Satan promises to give all power over this great civilization and all the kingdoms of the world to Christ, if Christ will fall down and worship him. The Son of God is unmoved by all "this grandeur and majestic show of luxury." And, as for Satan's offer, Christ answers with disdain, "I never lik'd thy talk, thy offer less . . . ." He adds that "It is written / . . . thou shalt worship the Lord thy God . . . / And dar'st thou to the Son of God propound / To worship thee accurst, now more accurst / For this attempt bolder than that on Eve and more blasphemous?"

Satan will not give up easily. He now poses another temptation to the Christ and this time he shows a panoramic view of Greek civilization which exemplifies intellectual power and glory. What a brillant evocation of wisdom is felt in the eloquent descriptions of Greece! To Satan's offer of the mastery of Greek wisdom and literature Jesus responds by showing the tremendous contrast between intellectual power and glory and spiritual power and glory.

Perhaps the dialogue between Christ and Satan on the wisdom of the Greeks should be carefully examined, for some of the arguments offered by Christ have caused certain critics to hold that the aging Milton, in contrast to the young Milton, is scorning intellectual excellence. This does not seem to be an accurate conclusion. Milton does note the inferiority of Greek to Hebrew philosophy and literature. Why? Consider the Hebrew writing: "God is praised aright, and godlike men, / The Holiest of Holies, and his saints, / Such are from God inspired." And Milton says further, ". . . He who receives / Light from above, from the Fountain of Light / No other doctrine needs. . . ." Is Milton contemptuous of Greek learning? It seems rather that he is stating cogently that the Greeks lacked true illumination because they did not have

"Light from above" and did not know the "Fountain of Light."
Actually in opposition to military, political and intellectual power
and glory, Milton places spiritual power and glory as superior.
There is really no change in Milton's basic philosophy. He says
practically the same thing regarding true glory in his early poem,
"Lycidas," (particularly in the passage on fame) as he says in this
disputed passage in a later work.

Paradise Regained now moves rapidly to its finish. Satan, frus-
trated and furious, leads Christ back to the wilderness. Night
comes, and Christ finds His sleep disturbed. Satan tries to upset
Christ with ugly dreams, "a night of storm and hellish furies."
The following morning Satan appears before Christ again and
presents his final temptation. He brings Christ to a pinnacle of
the temple, on which he sets Him. To stand on that pinnacle "will
ask thy skill." If He cannot stand, then Satan wants Him to cast
Himself down and ask God to give His angels charge over Him.
Jesus stands. And Satan falls "whence he stood to see his Victor
fall." A band of angels bear the victorious Christ from the pinnacle of the temple and take Him to a valley where all manner
of food and drink are placed before Him. As Christ refreshes
Himself, angelic choirs sing anthems of His victory "over temptation and the Tempter proud."

Christ then receives praise as the Victor over the temptations
of Satan; but His work is not over, for embedded within this hymn
is not only a picture of One who has completed a colossal task,
but also of One whose mission on earth has just begun. At the
close of the hymn, Milton says:

> Queller of Satan, on thy glorious work
> Now enter and begin to save mankind.

SAMSON AGONISTES (1671)

For this work Milton employed the form of Greek tragedy. In
fact, to Milton tragedy as a literary form inevitably implied Greek
tragedy rather than the forms developed by the Elizabethan and
Jacobean dramatists. These latter dramatists, so Milton says in
the preface, made the "error of intermixing comic stuff with tragic
sadness and gravity; or introducing trivial and vulgar persons."

Though the literary form of *Samson Agonistes* is Greek, most
of the characters are Hebraic, drawn from the book of Judges

(chapters 13-16). Beginning with a prologue, the tragedy contains a series of dialogues between Samson and the various individuals who visit him, with intervening soliloquies by Samson, comments by the chorus and the reported account of Samson's death.

Milton's theme is once more the familiar subject of temptation. Each character of the play "tempts" Samson, and in his overcoming of each temptation the reader senses the recovery of a despairing man to the status of a God-honoring hero.

The story of the play concerns the last day in the life of Samson, and the prologue establishes the fact of Samson's being blind and a prisoner of the Philistines, "eyeless in Gaza, at the mill with slaves." It is a holiday, and Samson is released for the day from his heavy labors. The people are holding a feast to their god, Dagon.

Samson comes forth into the open air, bemoaning his condition and lamenting the contrast between "what once I was, and what am now." As the chorus enters—a group of former friends—they, too, speak of the great difference between what Samson *was* and what he *is*. Commenting upon the entrance of the chorus, David Daiches points out that they speak first in tones of exaggerated quiet, appropriate to someone entering a sick chamber: "This, this is he; softly a while / Let us not break in upon him. . . ." Then as the chorus looks upon Samson, the contrast between his present state and former glory is borne in upon them, and the tone of their chant becomes passionate with shock and incredulity: "Or do my eyes misrepresent? Can this be he? / That Heroic, that Renowned / Irresistible Samson?"

As in Greek drama, the chorus plays an important role throughout Milton's *Samson Agonistes*. Among its most important functions are to interpret the emotions that are appropriate to succeeding developments of the action, to make clear the larger meaning of the play and to integrate the content of the entire drama.

When the chorus confronts Samson for the first time, they not only lament his fall, but want to know why he married a woman of the Philistines rather than someone of his own tribe. Samson muses over his relations with Dalila, whom he refers to as a monster, but then concludes, "She was not the prime cause, but I myself / Who vanquisht with a peal of words (O weakness!) / Gave up my fort of silence to a Woman."

Samson's first visitor is his old father Manoa. As Samson and the chorus have done earlier, Manoa laments the shocking change in Samson's position. His picture of Samson's present condition is vivid, but Manoa's comments carry a note of disappointment over what his son has become rather than genuine sympathy for Samson. Manoa also suggests that God is unfair for choosing Samson "to worthiest deeds" and then reducing him to such a humiliating state just because he erred "through frailty." At this point Samson tells his father not to rail against heaven, for he himself is the "sole author" and "sole cause" of the evils that have befallen him. As Manoa leaves, he is setting out to prosecute the means of a ransom for the deliverance of his son. Following his departure, the chorus and Samson ponder the baffling ways of God.

The Dalila scene follows. Decked out in all possible finery, Dalila approaches Samson hesitantly to be greeted with a fierce, "Out, out Hyena!" from Samson. But Dalila attempts to win Samson's forgiveness for her act of treachery in delivering him into the hands of his enemies. Her excuse is that out of love for Samson she wanted to keep him with her at home in her country. Many accuse her of lying and hypocrisy, but it seems wiser to believe that although she is capable of playing the hypocrite, she also has a distorted view of love. David Daiches says that Dalila is telling the truth when she gives her version of how and why she gave in to the Philistine lords. He contends that: "She wanted Samson at home and in her power. That was her way of loving him. It was a wrong way, but she is not lying in her account of it."[22] But when Samson rejects her offers, there seems to be no question but that she reveals herself as a treacherous woman, "who to save / Her country from a fierce destroyer, chose / Above the faith of wedlock bonds."

Samson's next visitor is Harapha, the Philistine bully and taunting braggart famous for brawn only. Harapha throws a number of indignities at Samson and brings before him the temptation of "trial by physical strength." Now Samson has reached the point where he can say that his strength is in the living God. After hearing the daring taunts of the physically limited and morally powerless Harapha for some time, Samson makes a pretended motion toward him and Harapha skulks from the stage.

A Philistine officer now enters and continues the "trial by physical strength." He summons Samson to appear before the Philistine lords in an exhibition of his strength at the festival in honor of Dagon. Undoubtedly the officer hopes that this will give the Philistines an opportunity to rub salt in Samson's wounds by their exulting publicly over the sad condition of their once dangerous foe. Replying to the officer with an emphatic, "I will not come," Samson, however, soon tells the chorus that for some time he has been aware that his physical strength is returning. Contemplating this growing strength and sensing a divine compulsion to go with the officer, Samson leaves in high dignity with him. As he leaves, he says to his friends of the chorus: "Happen what may, of me expect to hear / Nothing dishonorable, impure, unworthy / Our God, Our Law, my Nation or myself; / The last of me or not I cannot warrant."

Immediately following the departure of Samson, Manoa returns, happy in the success of his efforts to ransom his son and confident that he can secure his release. Manoa's speculation is interrupted by a messenger who relates that Samson has sacrificed his life for God in pulling down the pillars of the temple, thus causing the roof to fall on the Philistine assembly.

From that messenger one hears in detail all that Samson has said and done since he left the stage: feats of strength performed with incredible force; request for an intermission, as he leaned, as though tired, with both arms on the massy pillars that supported the arched roof; his final speech in which he reminded the Philistine lords that he had performed what their "commands imposed" and that he would subsequently show his strength, "yet greater"; and then the spectacular fall of the great temple as he drew the whole roof "with burst of thunder / upon the heads of all who sat beneath." Though Samson dies, he dies as a hero. Even Manoa recognizes the great tragic stature of Samson's death; for in his epitath for his dead son, he exultantly cries that "Samson hath quit himself / Like Samson, and heroically hath finished / A life heroic." Samson moves in the drama from a state of despair to the position of a heroic leader who recovered from his sense of failure and did God's work.

The play concludes with the echoes of a tremendous thought which has pervaded much of John Milton's writing:

> All is best, though we oft doubt,
> What th' unsearchable dispose
> Of Highest Wisdom brings about,

And ever best found in the close.
Oft He seems to hide his face,
But unexpectedly returns
And to his faithful Champion hath in place
Bore witness gloriously. . . .

EDWARD TAYLOR (1645-1729)

Born in England, Edward Taylor came to Colonial America as a young man and received his bachelor's degree from Harvard in 1671. He was a gifted Puritan poet as well as pastor and physician at Westfield, Massachusetts. His poetry remained unknown until the twentieth century since he did not allow its publication during his lifetime and requested that his heirs not publish it. In 1883 Henry Wyllys Taylor presented the four-hundred-page manuscript of his poetical works to Yale University. A specialist in American literature, Thomas H. Johnson, discovered the poems and requested permission from Yale to publish them. *The Poetical Works of Edward Taylor* were published in 1939. Writing somewhat in the style of the Metaphysical poets, Taylor left poems of remarkable intensity and striking imagery.

POETICAL WORKS

The *Poetical Works* consists of a verse sequence entitled "God's Determination Touching the Elect," a group of five occasional poems and selections from two series of "Sacramental Meditations."

"God's Determination," largely in dialogue form with Mercy, Justice, Christ, Satan, the Soul and a Saint as chief characters, embodies a contest between Christ and Satan for mankind. Coursing through the poem are long discussions of faith, grace and damnation. But the focus of Taylor's concern is the doctrine of redemption. The poet delineates the covenant God made with Adam thus: that he and his descendants would possess eternal happiness if they did not eat of the tree of the knowledge of good and evil. But Adam and Eve did eat of the fruit of the forbidden tree, and Taylor declares that through a new covenant of grace, man could still know eternal joy. If man would believe in Jesus Christ, who came into the world and died on the cross, he would know salvation. God's "determination" in bringing man to Himself may be seen in the passage in which Mercy replies to Justice concerning the respective destinies of Satan's and Christ's disciples:

> I will not only from his Sin him free,
> But fill with inherent grace also.
> Though none are Sav'd that wickedness embrace
> Yet none are Damn'd that have Inherent grace.

Of Taylor's occasional poems included in the *Poetical Works*, the most popular is "Huswifery," a poem of three six-line stanzas. Built upon the sustained images of the stages in manufacturing a robe of glory, Taylor asserts that when his understanding, will, affections, judgment, conscience, memory, words and action are dressed in this cloth woven by God, he would then be "cloathed in Holy robes for glory."

Edward Taylor's "Sacramental Meditations" contain some of his finest poetry. Written in the six-line stanza, rhyming *a b a b c c*, each meditation is numbered and based on a biblical text. Throughout the poems he uses highly figurative language and terms of earthly experience to convey his adoration of God. In the first of his "Sacramental Meditations" he depicts a consuming, passionate longing to be joined to God. His deep desire for the divine embrace is expressed in terms of earthly ceremony, but Taylor does not fail to distinguish sharply between the earthly experience and the experience of divine love. "Meditation Eight" attempts to discern in astronomy a link between heaven and man, but using the image of Christ as the bread of life, concludes that truth and sustenance are found only in Christ Jesus. In "Meditation Twenty" Taylor describes Christ's ascension into heaven and expresses his own longing for wings to follow Him.

Edward Taylor's poems are characterized by his celebration of the joys and deep delights of the Christian life. The Christian is bound for heaven, and ". . . in Christ's coach they sweetly sing, / As they to glory ride. . . ."

MISCELLANEOUS RELIGIOUS WRITINGS

The seventeenth century was a period which produced a variety of religious writings. There were numerous works that could probably be best classified as devotional manuals, meditations, letters and journals. Many of these writings are not known for their distinctively literary import, yet they are works that are not without some literary merit and are decidedly God-oriented in their thrust.

LANCELOT ANDREWES (1555-1626)

Lancelot Andrewes—who has become known to contemporary readers largely because of a study on him by T. S. Eliot—is the author of a devotional manual, *Private Devotions*, published after his death. Like others of the seventeenth century, Andrewes was keenly aware of man's inner needs and conflicts and he spends many pages on penitence, confession, worship and contemplation of God. Andrewes also never lost sight of the great truth that God reveals Himself in nature and in history, and he considered this cause for much serious reflection and sincere thanksgiving. Some of the most arresting sections of *Private Devotions* are the prayers of thanksgiving. Andrewes' series of *Seventeen Sermons on the Nativity* has also been widely acclaimed.

JOSEPH HALL (1574-1656)

Joseph Hall, the author of *Contemplations Upon the Principal Passages in the Holy Story*, was convinced that he had found a method of expounding scriptural truth different from the allegorical writings of the Church Fathers and the expositions of seventeenth century preachers. Consisting of one hundred forty-two meditations on Old Testament stories and forty-nine on stories from the New Testament, Hall's work found numerous readers and admirers. His *Meditations and Vows* demonstrates depth of spiritual insight on a variety of subjects. The three hundred meditations and vows vary in length from twenty to four hundred words.

FRANCIS QUARLES (1592-1644)

Little is known of the emblem writer Francis Quarles. He studied at Christ's College, Cambridge, was a member of Lincoln's Inn, and was attached to the court in the service of Princess Elizabeth. Author of numerous religious works in both prose and poetry, Quarles is best known as a composer of emblems. In its customary form, the emblem consists of three parts: a text from the Bible, a picture which interprets that text and a commentary in poetry or prose or both.

SAMUEL RUTHERFORD (*c.* 1600-1661)

The Scottish author Samuel Rutherford was rather prolific, but he lives among readers today primarily through his *Letters.* By far the greater part of the letters, two hundred fifteen out of two hundred eighty-six, came from one period of his life— the two years of enforced banishment from his Galloway parish to Aberdeen. As one would expect, the *Letters* vary in nature. Some are lamentations over the corruption in the church; some are letters of counsel and comfort; others are exhortatory, designed to provoke and promote growth; but all are filled with love and adoration for Christ. They strikingly illustrate what it means for an individual's soul to abide in God.

NICHOLAS HERMAN (*c.* 1605-1691)

Another devotional manual from the seventeenth century is one associated with Brother Lawrence (Nicholas Herman). The work, *The Practice of the Presence of God,* is not entirely his. Brother Lawrence wrote very little and destroyed most of what he did write. The superior of the Parisian monastery where Herman lived as a lay monk collected a few letters and fragments of meditation, supplemented these with notes from his own conversations and recollections, and thus gave posterity the picture of Brother Lawrence.

As the title suggests, the work depicts something of the manner in which Brother Lawrence literally practiced day by day the presence of God. Lawrence emphasized the need to dwell on the truth that God is everywhere present and that He is wise and merciful. When he first began to practice God's presence, he would plan his work so that he would have time to pray between jobs, but later he trained himself to talk to God while he was working. He so definitely felt that one should "pray without ceasing" that he came to believe it was a mistake to set off certain periods of time for prayer, for one should be "united to God by action, at the time of action, as by prayer in its time." Although he did not find it easy to rid his mind of distractions, Lawrence believed that by fixing the mind on God one could accustom himself to practice God's presence at all times. To Brother Lawrence, the practice of talking to God became a habit, and he rarely knew what it was like not to sense the presence of God.

Life was not all pleasantness for Brother Lawrence. He tells of some of his tasks that strike him as a bit trying, but contends that one can speak with candor to God about the unpleasant tasks and rely on Him for strength and grace. Practicing the presence of God did not mean that this lay monk lived a completely withdrawn life, however, for he took a sincere interest in the welfare of all in the monastery and demonstrated genuine charity toward those who came asking for alms. He was not one who enjoyed expressing his opinions on given questions, but when asked to do so, he spoke with perceptive judgment and "his answers were so clear . . . that they needed no comment." In time Brother Lawrence's reputation as a devout, discerning Christian became known beyond the monastery and numbers sought spiritual counsel from him.

BLAISE PASCAL (1623-1662)

A work which has been passionately read and discussed is *Pensées* by Blaise Pascal. When Pascal was thirty-one years of age he heard a sermon which made a profound impact upon him and became the seed of a deep religious experience. At the age of thirty-seven he conceived the plan of a great book which was to form a complete defense of the Christian faith—a work he did not live to finish. When he died in 1662 he left the voluminous, incisive notes or "thoughts" which constitute the book as it is known today.

Pascal's starting point is the greatness and misery of man and the necessity of man's knowing *who he is*. Setting forth in quest of self-knowledge, man compares himself with nature and discovers that he cannot comprehend his own nature by the same kind of knowledge through which he apprehends the world. Turning from external nature to the contemplation of the inward man, he discovers that man is a creature riddled with contradictions. He is a man of grandeur and a man of misery. He is created capable of knowing God, yet he is so corrupted that he does not know Him. Only in Christ can these diametrically opposed conditions be united, "for it is impossible to know Jesus Christ without knowing both man's misery as a sinner and his grandeur as a redeemed child of God. Christian faith acknowledges human weakness without falling into pride."[23] Yet if man is to be reconciled, then God must exist, and how does man know that God exists? After careful scrutiny of the human condition, Pascal is driven to offer his famous wager for the existence of God. Through the Wager Argument he seeks to prod "contradictory" man to place his life in God's hands. Pascal formulates the wager in terms of a forced option which presents an inescapable decision: If man believes in God, and if God does exist, he gains everything. If he believes and God does not exist, he loses nothing. On the other hand, if he disbelieves and God does exist, he loses everything; and if he disbelieves and God does not exist, he neither gains nor loses. Putting the wager in the most favorable light possible, ". . . it appeals to self-interest in order to force the complacent or skeptical man out of indifference. It breaks aside proofs and brings the discussion into the area of personal commitment. . . . Behind a pose of intellectual integrity, the doubter is actually incapable of surrendering his heart; he is annoyed that the basic questions of life call for decision . . . . The Argument seeks to break through the defense of this pose."[24]

As Pascal studied the great problems before him his conclusions can be summarized best by his own words, "Not only do we know God by Jesus Christ alone, but we know ourselves only by Jesus Christ. We know life and death only through Jesus Christ. Apart from Jesus Christ we do not know what is our life, nor our death, nor God, nor ourselves."

GEORGE FOX (1624-1691)

George Fox left what might be classified as a spiritual autobiography in *The Journal of George Fox*. In one sense the work is a journal in that one section describes Fox's travels in the West Indies and on the American continent. On the other hand, it is not a day-by-day account (nor does it profess to be) of his experience. Rather it is a remarkable story of the way God's power manifests itself and operates in the affairs of men (particularly through the overall experiences of one man). The *Journal* tells of an intense spiritual crisis Fox experienced in late adolescence through which he eventually discovered that the answer to his problems, the secret of spiritual triumph, lay in Christ. Believing that the presence of Christ in the individual's life and in the affairs of men was the basic need of all, he made no apologies for expounding his beliefs. By stating candidly his own convictions he often raised the wrath of those who disagreed with him. Sometimes this led to trials and imprisonment, and the *Journal·*

contains vivid descriptions of the interior of jails and the terrible discomforts to which prisoners were subjected. Fox also tells of the origin of the Society of Friends with its emphasis upon the vital, inward realities of Christian experience. He insists that man needs to learn to listen to the Spirit of Christ speaking to the individual heart. When one learns this, he will know what it means to live in the power of the Spirit.

Other aspects of Quaker belief are outlined, such as silent worship, the use of "thou" and the repudiation of violence. Although a definite age, people, and religious group are depicted, the principal picture is that of a sincere, honest man who believed that the power of God could transform lives and sustain man in the midst of any situation.

MADAME GUYON (1648-1717)

Madame Guyon is another of the numerous contemplative writers of the seventeenth century. Unhappy in her marriage and widowed at twenty-eight, she sought happiness and strength in the quietistic, devotional life. Madame Guyon's works run to forty volumes of several hundred pages each, but her best known book, *A Short and Easy Method of Prayer*, is probably the most familiar to modern readers. In this work she urges that men recognize prayer not as a formal offering up of specific requests or petitions, but as a spontaneous overflow of gratitude from a heart that is united to God in faith and love. Suggestions, like meditating on the various parts of the Lord's prayer, are offered for the development of "the true praying heart."

FRANÇOIS FENELON (1651-1715)

It was another French author who through his "letters of direction," according to Evelyn Underhill, reached and affected the eighteenth century Quakers, the leaders of the evangelical revival and the Tractarians."[25] This influential, ascetically inclined man was François Fénelon. His *Maxims of the Saints*, which gives spiritual direction on a variety of subjects such as prayer, meditation and adversity, shows the deep devotional aspect of his life and writings.

Though Anglican and Puritan authors produced the bulk of seventeenth century religious literature, no one group or movement monopolized the field. Catholics, Quakers and others diffi-

cult to label all gave significant depictions of man and his relation to God and the world.

Before moving to the study of the following century, some mention should be made of what Hardin Craig calls "the most perfect
monument of the age"—the King James Version of the Bible. Dr.
John Reynolds, president of Corpus Christi College, Oxford, suggested at the Hampton Court Conference in 1604 that work begin
on the new translation. Forty-seven leading scholars and preachers of the day were chosen as translators. The work took three
and a half years, and the King James Version of the Bible was
completed and published in 1611. To evaluate the dimensions of
its influence is impossible, yet "its literary influence is as com-
monplace, as is its influence on the English language and on . . .
thought."[26]

CHAPTER 3

The Eighteenth Century

THE EIGHTEENTH CENTURY introduced new patterns of thought in Western civilization. Often labeled the Age of Reason, the eighteenth century gave preponderant importance to the power of man's unaided intellect to open the doors to truth. It was a period of intellectual optimism and boundless faith in science. Abandoning supernatural premises, the eighteenth century thinkers practically deified man's reason, developed the idea of progress and increasingly broke away from a God-oriented point of view. The application of the new rationalism to religion did not exclude a belief in God. Instead the transcendent yet immanent God was replaced by a nonpersonal "god," who set in motion the universe and then left the scene, allowing the "rational machine" to pursue its own course. The influence of this viewpoint in all areas, including literature, is almost incalculable. Generally speaking, the literary men of the eighteenth century (particularly the first part of the period) had little interest in the concerns of the individual. They were far more interested in laws of conduct for man in society. With their rationalistic view of man and the world, they often used satire as a form of expression, for this was an excellent means for attacking people or institutions not conforming to the "general rules" for living in a rationalistic society. At the same time, the temper of the times was so hostile to the great mysteries of the Christian faith and to the individual's personal encounter with God that there was not a vast output of religious writing such as the seventeenth century produced. While there were no Donnes, Miltons or Bunyans in the eighteenth century, there were those who believed that the rationalism of the time did not provide the final answer to the meaning of life.

Some writers of religious literature made clear that faith was not antithetical to reason, but that the two were intertwined in discovering truth; others were concerned only with experiences conducive to the growth of the inner life; while yet others were preoccupied with the development of the inner self, but their chief concern was to give directions which would guide believers into more devout Christian living. But one does not find numerous distinctively creative works filled with the concern of the intimate relation between a human soul and his God. This is a period of many journals, polemical tracts, histories, diaries and treatises, some of which are of literary merit. It is a period, especially in American literature, of the sermon, a form which called forth the finest literary talent of the time. And there is some religious poetry which exemplifies the poet's artistic gift for depicting intensity of individual experience.

For the first time in the history of literature one can look to America for contributions of significance in religious writing. The seventeenth century, of course, saw the production of such work as Michael Wigglesworth's poem, "Day of Doom"—which is a kind of summary of Calvinistic theology—and the compilation of the *Bay Psalm Book;* but in the eighteenth century such men as Cotton Mather, Jonathan Edwards and John Woolman wrote works of quality and permanency.

COTTON MATHER (1663-1728)

Born in Boston in 1663, son of the Rev. Increase Mather and grandson of the Rev. John Cotton, Cotton Mather was one of the strongest Christian intellectuals of early New England. At eleven, according to some accounts, he wrote and spoke Latin with great facility, had gone through most of the New Testament in Greek and had begun his Hebrew grammar. When he received his Bachelor of Arts degree from Harvard in 1678 he was fourteen, the youngest graduate then on record. He thought of becoming a physician but later concluded that he should enter the ministry. After taking his Master of Arts degree in 1681, he assisted his father at the Second or Old North Church and became co-minister in 1685. Cotton Mather preached thousands of sermons and wrote untiringly. There are more than four hundred published items of which he is author, and great quantities of material are still extant in manuscript. Sermons, biographies, theological treatises, essays, handbooks for church members, letters, poems and various other types constituted his great bulk of writing.

Cotton Mather's most significant writings were designed primarily to stem the tide of decadence among Christians in New England churches and to remind them of their rich Christian heritage. His vast work *Magnalia Christi Americana* illustrates this design.

MAGNALIA CHRISTI AMERICANA (1702)

Believing that the rising generation of New England stood in danger of neglecting its heritage, Cotton Mather sought to bring it back to the principles that had characterized its founders. He held up before this new generation the memory of the great men who under God helped establish the New World, and exhorted that these men should be imitated and the godly principles for which they stood should be reinvigorated among New Englanders.

The work itself is not easy to classify for it is a collection of essays, memorials and addresses, all designed to show that New England owes its origin to the favor of Almighty God. Even though Satan used every conceivable tactic to hinder the foundation of New England, Mather reminds his readers that God not only selected the location, but He also prospered the building of this "wilderness Jerusalem." The new generation must never forget what God had wrought!

The "great American deeds of Christ," as the title suggests, are described by Cotton Mather in seven books encompassing: (1) an account of the settlement of New England; (2) the lives of the governors; (3) the lives of the ministers; (4) an account of Harvard College and its leaders; (5) acts and monuments of the New England churches (and this book sometimes is called the hub around which the rest of the work turns); (6) "Illustrious Discoveries and Demonstrations of the Divine Providence"; (7) and a description of "disturbances given to the Church of New England." The first four books are concerned primarily with praise for New England's great men. The fifth concerns the acts and monuments or doctrines and practices of the New England churches; and the final two books vividly show the demonstrations of divine favor as well as Satan's attempts to thwart God's work.

In praising the founders of New England, Mather often drew from his vast knowledge of classical literature for comparisons, sometimes to the unjustified decrease in stature of the classical figure. For example, when Mather compares John Winthrop, governor of Massachusetts, with Lycurgus, the Greek lawgiver, and Numa, the Roman lawgiver, he says: "Our New England shall tell and boast of her *Winthrop,* a lawgiver as patient as Lycurgus, but not admitting any of his criminal disorders; as devout as Numa, but not liable to any of his heathenish madness; a governor in whom the excellencies of Christianity made a most improving addition unto the virtues, wherein even without *those* he would have made a parallel for the great men of Greece, or of Rome, which the pen of a Plutarch has eternalized."

The praises and biographies of New England's great leaders are usually brief, but Mather's story of Sir William Phips in his progress from shepherd boy to shipbuilder and briefly as governor, runs for more than sixty pages. Perhaps the lengthiness of Phips' biography can be partially explained by Mather's inclusion of an account of the witchcraft trials that occurred during Phips' administration. There was no doubt in Mather's mind concerning the prevalence of witchcraft in New England, but he believed that caution should be exercised in bringing to trial and condemning to death those accused of demon possession.

From the literary point of view, Book Six is probably Mather's most creative. Splendid use of narrative and description are obvious in his account of the many demonstrations of God's providence and mercy in the lives of early New England founders. But perhaps just as vivid is his depiction of the disturbances and problems which the New England churches encountered in those early years. Particularly concerned with the "heresy" which the churches fought, Mather writes especially of Roger Williams, whom he considered to be a narrow separatist, and of Anne Hutchinson, an Antinomian. In its denial of any authority beyond the individual, Antinomianism struck at the heart of one of the basic concepts of the early Puritans and of Mather—their view of the Bible as God's revelation and His final authority for man. The Antinomian controversy ended for the most part with the banishment of Anne Hutchinson from the Bay Colony. Regardless of Anne Hutchinson's serious faults, Mather's denunciation of her, charging her with lying and bearing tales, seems a bit contemptuous and hard.

Cotton Mather seems to have had mixed views on the Quakers.

At one point he called them lunatics and warned the colonies to guard against "the dangerous villains," but on the other hand, he felt that their influence could be curbed through minor punishments, such as shaving off their hair.

At the end of the work Mather includes a discernible note of the need for toleration, but he boldly declares that because the opponents of Calvinistic theology and of the New England churches had not been successful, their next best move would be to try another religion.

Cotton Mather's *Magnalia Christi Americana*, still considered one of colonial America's great books, is a vast storehouse of information on early New England. The narrative is interspersed with quotations and allusions which exemplify the workings and strong convictions of a great mind.

Mather's serious attempt to clarify the relevance of Christian truth in all areas of life is evidenced in other works, such as *The Christian Philosopher*, which declared that science was an incentive to, rather than an enemy of, religion; and *Essays to do Good*, which demonstrated intense interest in scientific and philanthropic movements.

The style of most of Mather's writings is ornate and literally filled with allusions. To read his works demands time and thought, for they are packed with solid information, not only of his age, but of many ages, and they contain penetrating insights into the thinking and character of a great Puritan.

JONATHAN EDWARDS (1703-1758)

Jonathan Edwards has the reputation of being the greatest theologian America has produced, and of possessing one of the most original minds in this country's history. "By uniting a passionate love for God and His authority with a genius for logic and system, he made himself the foremost interpreter of Calvinism in America; and he has remained, down to the present day, a great bulwark of religion through his powerful affirmation of faith in the reality . . . of spiritual experience."[1]

Born at East Windsor, Connecticut, where his father was a minister, Edwards received his early education at home and later at Yale College, graduating before he was seventeen. Spending two additional years studying theology at Yale, and after an eight-month interval of serving as minister in a Presbyterian church

in New York City, Edwards tutored for three years at Yale. In
1727 he joined his grandfather in the church at Northampton,
Massachusetts, and became full minister of the church after his
grandfather died in 1729.

As a minister Jonathan Edwards became very interested in the
Great Awakening which began to reach New England by the
1730's. In fact partially through the power of his sermons the
Great Awakening spread over America. He welcomed the Awakening and helped reinvigorate the spiritual lives of believers as
did Increase and Cotton Mather. Because of his insistence that
individuals have a personal relationship with Christ before he
would admit them to communion and because of his return to
the straight preaching of first generation Puritans, Edwards was
dismissed as pastor of the church at Northampton. For about
six years, or until 1757, Edwards served as pastor at Stockbridge,
Massachusetts, and then became president of Princeton University
(then called the College of New Jersey). However, he died of
smallpox after only a few weeks in office.

Edwards wrote voluminously, and several of his works are
often included in anthologies of American literature. His sermons,
particularly, "A Divine and Supernatural Light" and "Sinners in
the Hands of an Angry God," are excellent examples of the sermon as a highly developed colonial literary type. They are also
illustrative of Edwards' attempt to explain clearly and logically
the teaching of particular Scripture texts and their application
to the need of the soul. Designed chiefly to persuade men to consider honestly the state of their souls, Edwards' sermons spoke
loudly to the individual mind, heart and will.

A TREATISE CONCERNING RELIGIOUS AFFECTION

A Treatise Concerning Religious Affection is considered an out-
standingly influential piece of Edwards' religious writing. His
statement that the affections are "no more than the vigorous and
sensible exercises of the inclination and will of the soul" is strong
support for those who would call Edwards as much a devotional
as an analytical writer. With the predominant thesis that true
religion consists in great part of holy affections, Edwards seeks
to resolve the question of how true religion can be distinguished
from false. He admits that true religion consists in great part
of the affections, but that it is by no means a subjective matter.

In light of his definition of affections he points out the signs of true religion: godly fear; hope in God, Christ and mankind; hatred of sin; holy joy and religious sorrow; gratitude; compassion; mercy; and zeal. But of all the affections, love is primary. It is the "fountain of all other affections," and the highest expression of love; and the "perfect example of true religion" is Jesus Christ.

Edwards goes on in Part Two to give twelve signs or distinguishing marks of true religious affections. Briefly, they are spiritual; they are founded on the excellence of divine things, not out of self-love, but for their own sakes; they are based on the *moral* excellency of divine things; they arise from the mind's *understanding* of divine things; they grow from a certainty based on the truth of the gospel; they are attended by an "evangelical humiliation" which shows an awareness of insufficiency without God's help; they demonstrate a change of nature; they promote the spirit of love, meekness, mercy and forgiveness; they exemplify a Christian tenderness of spirit; they exhibit symmetry and proportion in their affections; they show an increased spiritual appetite; and they result in a life of "Christian practice!" Edwards leaves no doubt that true and false religion can be distinguished by the difference in the individual's life. A true Christian commits his whole being to God, and this commitment manifests itself in Christian practice.

Freedom of the Will is another of Edward's rather popular works. Upholding his belief in a sovereign, omniscient God, he maintains at the same time that man has power of choice and must assume responsibility for his behavior.

Perhaps one of the most widely loved works of Jonathan Edwards is his spiritual autobiography, or his account of "his new sense of things," *Personal Narrative.*

PERSONAL NARRATIVE (written sometime after 1739)

Edwards' analytical mind is obviously at work in the *Personal Narrative* as he takes apart his youthful and his more mature spiritual experiences and reports his findings. But the great impact of this work is the insight one receives into a human soul literally longing for and finally finding deep, satisfying communion with God. Also, Edwards is deliberately seeking to put into practice those "religious affections" that distinguish the man of true religion from the man of the false.

Edwards begins by telling of one remarkable "season of awakening" which he experienced before his college days at the time of a great revival in his father's congregation. He states that for many months he was "much affected" by the experience. He prayed in secret five times daily and spent much time in "religious talk" with other boys. Desiring a place to retire for prayer, Edwards, along with some of his schoolmasters, built a booth in a deeply secluded swamp. His affection, he said, seemed to be lively and easily moved, and he was in his element when engaged in religious duties. Edwards closes his account of that early religious awakening with the statement: "And I am ready to think, many are deceived with such affections; and such a kind of delight as I then had in religion, and mistake it for grace." In process of time Edwards' early convictions and affections wore off, and he "returned like a dog to his vomit, and went on in the ways of sin."

During the latter part of his college days Edwards became ill with pleurisy, and God brought him "nigh to the grave" and "shook" him "over the pit of hell." Recovering from the illness, he soon returned to his old ways of sin, but he had no peace. He wanted a calm for his inner conflicts and struggles which were becoming more and more persistent. He had wrestled even as a child with the doctrine of God's sovereignty, and finally after years of struggling was convinced that the doctrine was scriptural. But in later years as he looked back upon his decision he realized that at the time he did not think of his conviction as proof of "any extraordinary influence of God's spirit." He rested in his acceptance of the doctrine, and some years after it was formed in his mind, it "appeared exceeding pleasant, bright, and sweet."

Edwards begins now to recall the various stages of thought and experience through which he passed until he was caught up with a keen awareness of the presence of God in his soul. His first instance of that "sort of inward, sweet delight in God and divine things" came subsequent to his reading I Timothy 1:17: "Now unto the King eternal, immortal, invisible, the only wise God, be honour and glory for ever and ever. Amen." As he read those words, there came into his soul a sense of the glory of the divine being: "a new sense," quite different from anything he had experienced before.

He then spent much time in reading and meditating upon Christ—His Person and the way of salvation through Him. He loved to read the whole book of Canticles (Song of Solomon) and dwelt particularly upon the verse, "I am the rose of Sharon, and the lily of the valleys" (2:1). Unable to explain what was happening in his soul, Edwards simply referred to the experience as ". . . a calm, sweet abstraction of soul from all the concerns of this world . . . sweetly conversing with Christ, and wrapt and swallowed up in God."

Soon Edwards discussed his new condition with his father and said only that he was affected by their discourse. But following the conversation Edwards walked alone in his father's pasture, exalted with a realization that in God are conjoined majesty and grace. Edwards was a *new* man, and he says that from that day in his father's pasture "my sense of divine things gradually increased, and became more and more lively. . . . There seemed to be . . . appearance of divine glory in almost everything." Yet he was not completely satisfied.

He was sure that he had experienced God's grace in his soul, but he still desired to know more of God. He spent much time alone in the woods and in solitary places, passing hours in meditation and prayer. He longed intensely for an answer to the question of how he could be more holy. There was constant self-examination and continual studying and contriving for ways to achieve greater conformity to the image of Christ. As Edwards looked back upon this stage of his experience, he admitted that he depended too much upon his own strength. But he persisted in his pursuit "after more holiness, and conformity to Christ." One of Edwards' most beautiful descriptions in the *Personal Narrative* is a picture of what he believed holiness did for the soul: ". . . it made the soul like a field or garden of God, with all manner of pleasant flowers; all pleasant, delightful, and undisturbed; enjoying a sweet calm, and the gently vivifying beams of the sun."

Edwards' sense of past sins also began to bother him. He sometimes wept at length as he reflected on how late in life he "began to be truly religious." Finally after much longing and wrestling, Edwards records this statement: "On January 12, 1723, I made a solemn dedication of myself to God, and wrote it down; giving up myself, and all that I had to God; to be for the future in no respect my own . . . and solemnly vowed to take God for my whole portion and felicity."

Admitting that he had often failed in his Christian walk, Edwards tells of his new delights in Christ. Conversations with godly people, hours alone with God and the Bible, contemplations of God's attributes—especially His holiness and His sovereignty, and reflections on ways of spreading the gospel—gripped his soul. The awareness of Christ became more real than ever before. Referring to his being "swallowed up in Christ," Edwards recalls the occasion on which he rode out into the woods near Northampton for a time of meditation and prayer. After alighting from his horse, he had a vision of the glory of Christ, of His grace, love, meekness, gentleness, and of His role as Mediator between God and man. In describing this experience Edwards writes, "The person of Christ appeared ineffably excellent with an excellency great enough to swallow up all thought and conception . . . which continued as near as I can judge, about an hour; which kept me the greater part of the time in a flood of tears, and weeping aloud."

As Jonathan Edwards looked into the inner recesses of his soul, analyzed the stages of his inner growth and reported his findings, he concluded in a note of triumph during another exalting experience: "I had . . . a very affecting sense, how meet and suitable it was that God should govern the world, and order all things according to His own pleasure; and I rejoiced in it, that God reigned, and that His will was done."

In the spring of 1755 Edwards began work upon two manuscripts representing the culmination of his private meditations. It is believed that he worked on these for the three remaining years of his life, but still considered them unfinished. The works were published after Edwards' death as *Two Dissertations: The Nature of True Virtue and Concerning the End for Which God Created the World*. These fragments are often thought of as an "unfinished summa," and a few scholars consider these to be Edwards at his greatest. The spontaneity, the perfection of form, and the probing of the soul's inner beauty of *The Nature of True Virtue* have caused the fragment to receive high praise from literary scholars.

Jonathan Edwards was a great thinker and artist. Although many of his works are of a polemical nature, he still speaks to the basic need of the human condition, not only as a theologian, but as an artist. Perry Miller calls Edwards "one of America's five or six major artists, who happened to work with ideas instead of with poems or novels." Miller continues, "He was much more a psychologist and a poet than a logician, and though he devoted his genius to topics derived from the body of divinity—the will, virtue, sin—he treated them . . . as problems not of dogma but of life."[2]

Calvinism as expressed by Cotton Mather and Jonathan Edwards remained a powerful force in America throughout the eighteenth century, and revivalism flourished at intervals throughout the period. Quakerism, too, found one of its finest American exponents—John Woolman.

JOHN WOOLMAN (1720-1772)

John Woolman seemed to live with one major aim—to keep his eye on the inner light until his own being was completely intertwined with the Infinite. Born in Northampton, New Jersey, of a Quaker family, John Woolman lived there until he was twenty, receiving a slight education and learning to love the Quaker way of life in his family, the village school and the weekly meeting. He then went into a shop not far from his home and learned the tailor's trade. A considerable portion of his time, especially during the last half of his life, was spent visiting and testifying at Quaker meetings and in Quaker homes. In 1772 he went to England attempting to arouse Quakers to a new sense of responsibility, not only for their own inner lives but also for social needs. He died in York, England, in 1772.

John Woolman wrote more than a dozen essays on matters which he considered to be of particular concern to Quakers, but it is his *Journal*, published posthumously, which gives him a distinctive place in American literary history.

JOURNAL (1774)

"Get the writings of John Woolman by heart and love the early Quakers," wrote Charles Lamb in the *Essays of Elia*. Lamb is only one among many readers who are enthusiastic admirers of the *Journal*, of the man who wrote it and of the ideas for which the author stood.

External details of Woolman's life are of interest to a reader, but one soon discovers that these serve only as a framework for the unfolding of his inner, spiritual growth. In fact, the *Journal* begins with an account of his early sensitivity to a restless conscience. The earliest recorded experience of religious awareness is reminiscent of another spiritual classic, Augustine's *Confessions,* for Woolman tells of his needless and wanton killing of a mother robin and subsequently a regretted euthanasia of her young. This event and his resultant remorse led him to say: "I was early convinced in my mind that true religion consisted in an inward life, wherein the heart does love and reverence God the Creator, and learns to exercise true justice and goodness, not only toward all men, but also toward the brute creatures." Throughout the *Journal* is the pervading idea that the individual who genuinely loves God must love Him in all His manifestations in the visible world—in all living beings, animals as well as man.

Woolman was twenty-three years old when his apprentice master directed him to write out a bill of sale for a Negro woman. The spiritual aftermath of this event within his conscience led him to write that he "believed slave keeping to be a practice inconsistent with the Christian religion." Woolman never wrote another bill of sale for a Negro, and on numerous occasions when he was requested so to do, he spoke out so earnestly against the sale of human lives that other consciences were quickened by his sincere protest.

Much of Woolman's life was spent in travel throughout the colonies, speaking with his fellow Quakers, especially on the matter of keeping slaves, and later preaching to the Indians. As he traveled, particularly in the southern colonies, he became more and more concerned about the unnecessary luxury of those who had slaves, the often less-than-humane conditions of the slaves and the continuing importation of Negroes in the slave traffic.

Particularly impressive is his absolute consistency in the matter of social justice as he saw it. In his southern travels he paid Negro servants who attended him, in spite of extremely limited personal means, meanwhile being as tactful as possible about the matter with their masters. In another instance, though it was to his disadvantage civilly and socially, he refused to pay taxes for the purpose of a war directed against the Indians. On one occasion while he was in England, though he was without a horse, he refused to utilize a stagecoach either for riding or for post because the children employed to drive were ill-treated and the hapless horses were pushed often to the point of death.

He traces many social evils, especially slavery, to the love of outward, material, superfluous things. An incident particularly indicative of his opinions is the record of his meeting with a colonel in the South, who told him that the Negro was congenitally slothful, and that, considering how badly they lived in Africa, they had no right to complain. Another encounter exposed Woolman to the weak scriptural hermeneutics that the Negro deserves mistreatment because he bears the mark of Cain. Woolman's reflection is worthy of record: "The love of ease and gain are the motives in general of keeping slaves, and men are wont to take hold of weak arguments to support a cause which is unreasonable." Woolman was by no means opposed to material gain, but he did hold that when it is acquired at the expense of one of God's creatures, the Creator cannot possibly approve.

Perhaps the earmark of the content of Woolman's *Journal* is his sense of inescapable personal responsibility for the inequities and unwise living that affected and afflicted his fellow creatures. Behind this was the firm conviction that one should live according to the "inner light" of his own conscience regardless of what others might think of his practices. And Woolman was just as positive that if men would only listen for the "inner voice" they would hear it clearly and unmistakably. He believed, as he stated it, that men could "get down to the Rock, the sure Foundation, and there hearken to that divine Voice which gives a clear and certain Sound."

Though many details crowd Woolman's *Journal*, his style is lucid and the work is of artistic merit. It is sprinkled liberally with Scripture and cites the need for appropriating biblical truth in day-to-day living.

John Woolman was one of the few eighteenth century Quakers to leave a full and revealing account of his amazingly sensitive inner life. And because he "never forgot our common humanity his *Journal* remains a living testament to a great man and a continuing challenge to mankind."[3]

WILLIAM LAW (1686-1761)

Born into the family of a prosperous businessman in King's

Cliffe, Northamptonshire, William Law attended Emmanuel College, Cambridge, and in 1711 became a fellow there. After the death of Queen Anne and the ascension to the throne of the Hanoverian prince as George I, holders of academic and ecclesiastical offices were required to take oaths of allegiance to the new monarch. Because William Law refused to swear allegiance to George I, he lost his post at Emmanuel College and was debarred from church appointments. For several years he tutored the son of Edward Gibbon, grandfather of the renowned historian. In 1740 he retired to King's Cliffe where he passed the remainder of his life. During these years he was occupied with his writing, served as spiritual director of two pious and congenial women, who supervised a school he had founded, and dispensed charity to the poor.

Although William Law was a Nonjuror, he was never closely associated with the Nonjuring groups. His writings, particularly his treatise on *Christian Perfection,* and to a greater extent his *Serious Call,* had a significant influence on John Wesley, George Whitefield and other Evangelicals, but Law himself was never in the same camp as these great Christian leaders. Yet Law appears to be deeply concerned in awaking all Christians to the implications of their faith. A work which unquestionably unfolds this deep concern is his *Serious Call,* published in many editions and to this day considered a religious classic.

A SERIOUS CALL TO A DEVOUT AND HOLY LIFE (1728)

"This was the first occasion of my thinking in earnest of religion after I became capable of rational inquiry." These are the words of Samuel Johnson after reading *A Serious Call to a Devout and Holy Life* while he was a student at Oxford. After reading this book Johnson was convinced that it was possible to be a Christian without any loss of intellectual integrity.

As recently as 1951 a group of men from different walks of life met each Wednesday noon in the kitchen of the First Presbyterian Church of Fort Wayne, Indiana, and read and studied *A Serious Call.* Each man purchased a copy of the work and read it in his leisure. When they came together as a group, one would read aloud until someone interrupted with a comment. Some days they would read an entire chapter without interruption, and other days only a sentence or two. As the weeks passed and the group

grew larger, the response of the men to *A Serious Call* was that
". . . we came to feel that William Law was one of our number.
He seemed to speak directly to us!"⁴

There is no question concerning the *Serious Call's* being po-
tentially capable of speaking to all, for to William Law every individual is called to devote his life to God, and he directly addresses people from all stations of life.

One of Law's first clarifications is that prayer is an important
part of a devout life, but: "Devotion is neither private nor public
prayer, but a life given to God. He is the devout man, therefore,
who considers and serves God in everything and who makes all
of his life an act of devotion by doing everything in the name of
God." To William Law the devout life means practicing Christian ideals in every little detail of life, and if the Christian does
do this, there is little reason for spending time in prayer. A holy
life means the dedication to God of all one is, and possesses—his
time, money, and abilities. Whatever an individual does must
also be governed by the teaching of Scripture—with the awareness
that he is to do all to the glory of God.

Early in his book Law raises the question of why the lives of
some avowed Christians are "strangely contrary to the principles
of Christianity." His emphatic answer is that many Christians
simply never intended to live holy lives. "It was the general in-
tention," wrote Law, "that made the primitive Christians such
eminent examples of devotion, that made the goodly fellowship
of the saints, and that made all the glorious army of martyrs and
confessors. And if you will stop here and ask yourself why you
are not so devoted as the primitive Christians, your own heart will
tell you that it is neither through ignorance nor inability but
purely because you never thoroughly intended it." Law is convinced that the multiple imperfections and "disorders" of the daily
lives of Christians can be explained in one way: "We have not so
much Christianity as to intend to please God in all the actions of
our life."

Law is unafraid to stress the place of reason in Christian living,
but he does so without minimizing scriptural authority. Having
posited his conviction that one must *intend* to live a devout life,
Law goes on to discuss definite precepts for the cultivation of
true piety. As previously stated, Law believes all individuals are
called to a devout and holy life and he applies his "rules" to *all*.

But on the other hand he gives far more space to practical suggestions for those of rank and high station. He has much to say to those of wealth and leisure. "If we waste our money," writes Law, "we are not only guilty of wasting a talent which God has given us, but we do ourselves this further harm: we turn this useful talent into a powerful means of corrupting ourselves." Law does not consider the possession of riches evil, but he warns against the "indiscreet use" of money and estates and of the buying and selling of houses and lands.

The privileged class is responsible also for the wise use of leisure: time as well as money must be spent not only in improving one's own soul, but also in helping others to improve theirs. People of leisure and fortune are those who are recipients of five talents. Consequently, Law says to these, ". . . it is now your duty to turn your five talents into five more. It is your duty to consider how your time and leisure and health and fortune may be so many happy means of purifying your own soul, improving your fellow creatures in the way of virtue, and carrying you at last to the greatest heights of eternal glory." Among the suggestions which Law delineates for accomplishing these high purposes are solitude, prayer, reading, meditation, singing psalms and hymns and reflecting frequently upon future glory. He also emphasizes "charitable activity," citing Matthew 25:31-46 as the basis for his injunction. And Law apparently believes that charitable acts should be done for those who seemingly are in need—without scrutinizing the details of their circumstances. He praises, for example, the judgment and action of one woman, who always helps a beggar claiming to be in need of food or money, even though she does not know whether he is a cheat. Agreeing with the woman's thinking that she may often give to those who will make ill use of her alms, Law goes on to point up her reasoning: "Does not God make his sun to rise on the evil and on the good? Do I not beg God to deal with me according to his own great goodness rather than according to my merit? Shall I, then, be so absurd as to withhold my charity from a poor brother because he may not deserve it? Shall I use a measure toward him which I pray God never to use toward me?" These rhetorical questions reflect the spirit in which charitable acts should be administered, according to William Law.

Although Law insists that the devout life means doing all things in the name of God, he also believes that one of the most essential means of cultivating the devout life is to pray. He gives a conspicuous place to the significance of the prayer life in *A Serious Call*. One should imitate the example of the early Christians and begin the morning with prayer. And these early morning prayers should be *early*, for to Law, one of the great enemies of the devout life is "sloth," by which he primarily meant late sleeping. The habit of late sleeping makes one a "slave to bodily appetites," and gradually "wears away the spirit of religion and sinks the soul into a state of dullness and sensuality." At the early morning prayer times the individual should offer up the entirety of his being to God for His service and glory. Nine in the morning is a good time to pray for humility. At noon, the theme should be love, and one should pray especially for his fellowmen. At three one should pray for conformity to God's will, and at six one should confess his sin and acknowledge his shortcomings. Before retiring, the proper subject for meditation is death, for the worshiper should think of the bed as a symbol of the grave.

Law also spends some time on the form that prayers should follow and the manner in which one should come into God's presence. He contends that a form of prayer is very necessary and expedient for public worship, but if the worshiper can find a better way of "raising his heart unto God in private than by prepared forms of prayer," he does not object. However, Law does believe that even in private prayers, as a general principle one should follow a prepared form; but if "In the midst of his devotions, he finds his heart ready to break forth into new and higher strains of devotion, he should leave his form for a while, and follow those fervors of his heart, till it again wants the assistance of his usual petitions." Law recommends that before beginning his various prayer times, the worshiper first chant a psalm to clear the way for prayer. Psalms also "disperse dullness of heart," "purify the soul" from little passions and address the soul toward heaven.

One distinctive characteristic of Law's writing style is his use of character sketches. After making general statements he cites a character illustrative of his position and discusses his moral and religious qualities. For example, he makes a number of cogent statements on the right use of time and money, contending that anyone who wisely manages either one cannot long be ignorant of the right use of the other. He then cites two maiden sisters for character illustrations. Flavia has a small income which she spends mostly on dress, and by discreet management she outdoes many who have greater wealth. She is positive that all poor people are cheats and liars. She considers those who play cards on Sunday to be atheists, but as soon as she comes from church, she will relate "the nicety of all the games, what cards she held, and how she played them at a party the night before." Miranda, Flavia's sister, is an entirely different person. "As soon as she was mistress of her time and fortune," says Law, "it was her first thought how she might best fulfill everything that God required of her in the use of them, and how she might make the best and happiest use of this short life." She has but one reason for doing or not doing, for liking or not liking, anything—and that is the will of God. Law says that to tell the story of Miranda's charity would be to relate the history of every day for twenty years. He does tell how she helped set up tradesmen in business, educated several poor children and got them honest employment, paid laborers twice their wages during periods of illness, and showed compassion to common beggars—especially those who were old or sick.

There are many portraits in the *Serious Call*, some of them admirable in literary skill and effectiveness; others are overdrawn, delivering long, tedious, unconvincing deathbed speeches.

In the concluding chapter of *A Serious Call* William Law reiterates many of his thoughts in this succinct summary: "Any devout man makes a true use of his reason. He sees through the vanity of the world, discovers the corruption of his nature, and admits the blindness of his passion. He lives by a law that is not visible to vulgar eyes; he sets eternity against time; and he chooses rather to be forever great in the presence of God than to have the greatest share of worldly pleasure while he lives. He who is devout is full of these great thoughts."

WILLIAM COWPER (1731-1800)

During the last two decades of the eighteenth century a group of poets broke with the critical rules of the Age of Reason. By introducing new subjects, depicting a love for nature and all living creatures, and writing in simple diction and strong lyrics they helped usher in the Romantic movement of the nineteenth century. Among the precursors of this movement is William Cowper. But Cowper is not only a transitional poet or a pre-Romantic writer. In choosing to write moral satires and didactic verse; in his love for the classics; and in his taste for aphorisms, he is typical of his age. At the same time, he is distinctive as the one great poet of the Evangelical movement. He is probably best understood in relation to the Evangelical revival which came largely in the wake of eighteenth century preachers like George Whitefield and John Wesley.

William Cowper's father was rector of St. Peter's Church at Great Berkhampstead, Hertfordshire, and chaplain to George II. His mother, Anne Donne, was a descendant of the seventeenth century poet and Anglican preacher John Donne. Her death came when William Cowper was only six years of age, and late in life he admitted that not a day passed in which he did not think of her. His "On the Receipt of My Mother's Picture," written near the close of his life, pays a remarkable tribute to his mother.

Cowper attended Westminster School and studied law at Middle Temple. He fell in love with his cousin Theodora and wanted to marry her, but the marriage was thwarted by her father, who, according to some biographers, saw evidence of emotional instability or the beginnings of insanity in Cowper. Whether Theodora's father actually believed Cowper was mentally unbalanced may be a speculative matter, but it is a fact that the poet became so emotionally perturbed that he was put away in a private asylum. After careful treatment by his physician, Dr. Nathaniel Cotton, a man of deep religious convictions, Cowper was released from the doctor's care and took lodging with the Unwins in the village of Huntington.

In this household Cowper was fortunate; Morley Unwin was a clergyman and tutor, and Mrs. Unwin encouraged Cowper to write poetry. When Unwin died, the boarder remained in Mrs. Unwin's house with her son and daughter and moved with her to Olney, where John Newton was curate. Cowper became Newton's assistant and collaborated with him on *Olney Hymns.* Cowper's readers are indebted to the Unwins for their encouragement of the poet, but it was at the suggestion of a charming, rich widow, Lady Austen, that Cowper wrote his major work, *The Task.*

Gripped by periods of despondency and emotional upsets until his death in 1800, William Cowper still was able to leave a collection of reputable poems, hymns, letters and memoirs. A representative selection of his hymns and poems are considered here.

OLNEY HYMNS (1779)

At the suggestion of the Rev. John Newton, Cowper collaborated with him in composing and eventually publishing a collection of hymns. Each was to contribute approximately the same
number, but because Cowper's second bout with despondency
hampered his work, the *Olney Hymns* contained only sixty-seven
hymns by Cowper and two hundred eighty-one by Newton. Some
of the hymns express Cowper's conflict and doubt; others show
his faith and hope.

In a self-questioning spirit, Cowper could write:

> Where is the blessedness I knew
> When first I saw the Lord?
> Where is the soul-refreshing view
> Of Jesus and His Word?

But the poet also could express a strong assurance of personal
faith:

> E'er since by faith, I saw the stream
> Thy flowing wounds supply,
> Redeeming love has been my theme,
> And shall be till I die.

A few of Cowper's hymns, such as "Oh, for a Closer Walk with
God"; "God Moves in a Mysterious Way"; and "Hark, My Soul!
It is the Lord" contain excellent poetry and are among the most
famous hymns in the English language.

POEMS (1782)

The first volume of *Poems* included eight lengthy, didactic selections which did not depart far from eighteenth century standards. Occasionally they include flashes of spontaneity and nat-
uralness which are characteristic of the major Romanticists. But
his numerous aphorisms, his solemn moralizing and his skillful
satire indicate his absorption of the predominant tendencies of
his age.

The Rev. John Newton says of Cowper's *Poems*, "He aims to
communicate his own perceptions of the truth—beauty, and influence of the religion of the Bible,—a religion . . . which alone
can relieve the mind of a man from painful and unavoidable
anxieties, inspire it with stable peace and solid hope, and furnish

those motives and prospects which . . . are absolutely necessary to produce a conduct worthy of a rational creature. . . ."[5]

Almost every page of *Poems* contains overtones of the aim stated by Newton. In "Table Talk" Cowper expresses his regret that England is no longer the strong Christian nation that she once was. The depth of his concern becomes obvious in such foreboding, moralizing aphorisms as:

> When profanation of the sacred cause
> In all its parts, times, ministry, and laws,
> Bespeaks a land, once Christian, fallen and lost
> In all that wars against that title most;
> And regions long since desolate, proclaim:
> Nineveh, Babylon and Ancient Rome
> Speak to the present times and times to come. . . .

Cowper's concern is just as intense over the absence of a truly religious poet in England. Referring to the poetic gift as "The gift whose office is the Giver's praise / To trace Him in His word, His works, His ways," Cowper laments the abuse of poetic genius by England's poets who waste their time on subjects unworthy of their high calling.

"The Progress of Error" is literally filled with generalizations on moral living. Underlying his moralizing is a positive thesis that pleasures "admitted in undue degree enslave the will." But his condemnation of numerous specific pastimes depicts negative overtones. For example, Cowper censures a "pastor of renown" for fiddling on Sunday, and warns that the "sickliest sheep of every flock" may follow the example of their priest and abuse the "Sabbath hours." After all, Cowper reasons, "If apostolic gravity be free / To play the fool on Sundays, why not we?" And in deft satire the poet exclaims, "Strike up the fiddles! let us all be gay! / Laymen have leave to dance, if parsons play." Also receiving the brunt of Cowper's barbed attacks are philosophers, novelists and educators who corrupt the minds of youth.

"Truth" contains "Heaven's easy, artless, unencumbered plan" for man's salvation. "Believe and live" is the heart of Cowper's creed, for faith alone leads to eternal life and the "plea of works . . . Heaven turns from with abhorrence and disdain." Scripture is upheld as the source of man's growth. "The book shall teach you; read, believe, and live!" is Cowper's admonition. Central also in this poem is the belief in man's depravity and the significance of the atonement.

"Expostulation" is basically another plea for England to turn from its loose morals and empty religion to "the true God, the God of truth."

"Hope" proclaims the significance of hope and declares in Cowper's aphoristic fashion that "Life without hope can close but in despair." Yet all hope is, despair "that stands not on His [Christ's] cross."

"Charity" praises the plan of God in creating all men as brothers. Particular tribute is paid to John Thornton, an Evangelical and patron of John Newton, and to John Howard, a prison reformer. In this poem Cowper also denounces slavery: "Virtue dreads it as her grave."

"Conversation" is less preoccupied with precepts and doctrines of the Evangelical revival than are many of the works in Cowper's collection of *Poems.* Didactic in nature, "Conversation" stresses the need for honest, straightforward discussions on religion without wrangling, hypocrisy or gossip.

In "Retirement" he emphasizes the beauties of nature—an emphasis definitely prophetic of the Romantic era. But Cowper warns that: "Who studies nature with a wanton eye / Admires the work, but slips the lesson by." Cowper was concerned with the idea that loving nature is not incompatible with loving God. And perhaps what he wanted above all was to arouse and strengthen man's belief in God by helping him see God reflected in nature. To Cowper the spiritually enlightened perceive in nature a beauty and unity that escape non-Christians.

THE TASK (1785)

A long poem in blank verse, *The Task* contains six books on various subjects relating to Cowper himself, the wonder of nature, simple rural living, and domestic, social, ethical and moral issues.

Beginning in mock-epic style on the invention of the sofa, Cowper moves in Book I to a description of the gypsies, who contribute little to mankind's betterment, to an indictment of London. This great city, according to Cowper, is the center of philosophy and commerce, but fashion has superseded truth, and the absence of the fear of God is obvious. But the poet clearly enunciates:

God made the country and man made the town
What wonder then that health and virtue, gifts
That alone make sweet the bitter draught
That life holds out to all, should most abound
And least be threatened in the fields and groves?

In Book II of *The Task*, Cowper yearns for a "lodge in some vast wilderness" where he will not constantly hear of man's brutality to man and where questions of race and color will bear no relevance. Chastising England for her slaves abroad, the poet still passionately exclaims, "England, with all thy faults, I love thee still / My Country! . . ." And the second book closes with a plea for freedom wherever the flag of England waves.

The third book opens with an address to domestic happiness. The "only bliss of Paradise that has survived the fall!" Cowper contrasts domestic happiness with the evils of prostitution and infidelity, which he satirically associates with city life. Then, suddenly becoming introspective, Cowper writes:

I was a stricken deer that left the herd
Long since; with many an arrow deep infixed
My panting side was charged, when I withdrew
To seek a tranquil death in distant shades.
There I was found by One who had Himself
Been hurt by the archers. In His side He bore,
And in His hands and feet, the cruel scars.
With gentle force soliciting the darts,
He drew them forth, and heal'd, and bade me live.
Since then, with few associates, in remote
And silent woods I wander, far from those
My former partners of the peopled scenes;
With few associates and not wishing more.
Here much I ruminate, as much I may,
With other views of men and manners now
Than once, and others of a life to come.
I see that all are wanderers, gone astray
Each in his own delusions . . .
I sum up half mankind,
And add two-thirds of the remainer half,
And find the total of their hopes and fears
Dreams, empty dreams . . . .

The poet then explores the varieties of dreamers. The millions who live from one pleasure to the other as if "created only like the fly," and the "sober dreamers" who appear "grave and wise" but are "dropping buckets into empty wells, / And growing old in drawing nothing up." Turning again to the values of the rural world, Cowper makes clear that "friendly to the best pursuits of man" . . . "to thought, to virtue and to peace" is "Domestic life in rural leisure passed!"

Cowper's third book has been criticized for its narrow, with-drawing spirit, but there is obviously truth in the suggestion that "though a lofty detachment from the combat may, if long con-tinued, become a deadly danger in its turn, who . . . is not the better for surveying now and then the vanity of human wishes and for drawing from the vision, as Cowper proceeds to do, a fresh satisfaction in the plain duties, simple joys, and abiding consolations open to us all?"[6]

Book IV is an extremely poetic section. In simple beauty Cow-per depicts a peaceful evening in the home and cannot help con-trasting it with the unhappy and morally loose life of city dwell-ers. He remarks how pleasant it is to peep at that world through the "loopholes of retreat."

There follows a tribute to winter which Cowper describes as the "king of intimate delights," "fire-side enjoyments," "home-born happiness" and "all the comforts that . . . the hours of long, uninterrupted evening know." Cowper then discloses a moving tribute to evening, describing its soothing effects, the peace and calm found in reclining in front of the "glowing hearth" while the "rough winds endear the silence and the warmth enjoyed within!" The poet expresses regret that he did not live in those happy days of which Sidney writes when the world was an Arcadia. But he reflects that those "happier days" never really existed; Arcadia was the result of "the poet's hand imparting substance to an empty shade" and imposing "a gay delirium for a truth."

Cowper recognizes the fact that the pastoral retreat is not safe from the vices of the city. He realizes that man cannot always live away from society, but he regrets what society can do to the dignity of the individual. Consider his words:

> Man in society is like a flower
> Blown in its native bed: 'Tis there alone
> His faculties, expanded in full bloom,
> Shine out; there only reach their proper use.

> But man associated and leagued with man
> By regal warrant, or self-joined by hand
> For interest sake, or swarming into clans
> Beneath one head for purposes of war,
> Like flowers selected from the rest, and bound
> And bundled close to fill some crowded vase,
> Fades rapidly, and by compression marred,
> Contracts defilement not to be endured.

Cowper demonstrates that the individual realizes his own fullness only in society; however, regimentation of any kind mars his distinctiveness and his dignity. Closing Book IV with a romantic address to nature, Cowper reveals how he loved nature from his youth and rejoices that all men can enjoy the beauty and variety of God's work.

Book V opens with a description of the sights and sounds of nature in the morning, but Cowper broadens his perspective to include expressions of his faith in the freedom and liberty of all humanity. Moralizing on the crime of tyranny and the tortures of imprisonment, the poet then pens some of his best known lines:

> 'Tis liberty alone that gives the flow'r
> Of fleeting life its lustre and perfume;
> And we are weeds without it. All constraint,
> Except what wisdom lays on evil men,
> Is evil; hurts the faculties, impedes
> Their progress in the road of science; blinds
> The eyesight of discov'ry; and begets,
> In those that suffer it, a sordid mind
> Bestial, a meagre intellect, unfit
> To be the tenant of man's noble form.

As Cowper ponders the sober possibility of England's losing that "for which our Hampdens and our Sidneys bled," he concludes that no tyranny can destroy the "liberty of heart, derived from Heaven," for "He is the freeman whom the truth makes free." Thus the slave who can appreciate the beauties of God's works knows a liberty that his oppressor is unable to realize, unless he also knows God and appreciates nature. Cowper concludes Book V with an exhortation to those whose lives fail to possess the knowledge of God which enables man to appropriate "nature as his Father's work":

> Acquaint thyself with God, if thou wouldst taste
> His works. Admitted once to His embrace,
> Thou shalt perceive that thou wast blind before;
> Thine eye shall be instructed, and thine heart,
> Made pure, shall relish with divine delight,
> Till then unfelt, what hands divine have wrought.

In the final book of *The Task* Cowper pleads for all men to awaken to the wonders of creation. Urging that "nature is but a name for an effect whose cause is God," the poet earnestly stresses that nature should be "read" and understood as a revelation of God. But, even though the marvels of nature surround man, he fails to see these wonders. And Cowper wants to open men's eyes to their wonderful world. So in Book VI the poet unfolds the varieties of God's creation and seeks to show "the Lord of all . . . is the life of all that lives." His handiwork, says Cowper, is revealed in the operation of the planets, the changes of seasons, the instincts of animals, the variety of trees, the uniqueness of flowers. Of the latter he says there is not the most delicate flower "but shows some touch in freckle, streak, or stain of His unrivalled pencil." And that individual who perceives this world of nature as the work of God sees not only its beauty and variety, but also a creative Presence that adds new luster to its beauty. The poet expresses the concept in this way:

> Happy who walks with Him! Whom what he finds
> Of flavour or of scent in fruit or flower,
> Or what he views of beautiful or grand
> In nature, from the broad majestic oak
> To the green blade that twinkles in the sun,
> Prompts with remembrance of a present God.
> His presence, who made all so fair, perceived,
> Makes all still fairer.

Interspersing the final book with didacticisms on the effects of the fall of man on nature, Cowper affirms that "the shattered world" shall know a triumphant restoration, for "all were once perfect, and all must be at length restored. / So God has greatly purposed."

MISCELLANEOUS WRITERS

The eighteenth century produced a number of writers with penetrating spiritual insight and flashes of artistic ability. Although these writers were overshadowed by the "greater artistic lights," some deserve consideration.

PHILIP DODDRIDGE (1702-1751)

A devotional writer possibly known more widely for his hymns than for his prose is Philip Doddridge. He is the author of two greatly loved hymns, "Awake, My Soul, Stretch Every Nerve" and "O Happy Day that Fixed My Choice." Doddridge's chief religious work in prose is *The Rise and Progress of Religion in the Soul*, particularly designed to show the Christian in a vast range of circumstances and to point out those that hinder and those that promote spiritual growth.

JOHN WESLEY (1702-1791)

John Wesley left his spiritual autobiography in his *Journal*. This work stirs the minds and hearts of many readers with its sharp focus upon man's responsibility to live a holy life and to proclaim Christ's atonement to a world in need. In the *Journal* Wesley shows that the witness of the Holy Spirit in the heart may sometimes be accompanied by emotional expression, but he makes clear that the real evidence of the work of God is gleaned from the changes wrought in lives. Encouraging the gathering of Christians in small societies for their mutual growth, Wesley also urges that these groups show concern for the educational, economic and social needs of man. It is of interest to observe that the writings of Thomas à Kempis, Jeremy Taylor and William Law intensified his interest in spiritual matters.

Wesley's *Christian Perfection* is often considered one of the classic treatises on the devotional life. In it Wesley outlines detailed advice to those who would embrace the doctrine of perfection, which he defines as loving God "with all our heart, mind, soul, and strength."

SAMUEL JOHNSON (1709-1784)

Samuel Johnson is an English author particularly known for his monumental enterprise, the *Dictionary*, and for his literary criticism, *The Lives of the Most Eminent Poets*. He also wrote some works distinctively religious in nature. His sermons and prayers have a relevant place among the writings of religious literature.

JAMES HERVEY (1713-1758)

James Hervey, greatly influenced by Wesley, is another devotional writer of some merit in the eighteenth century. His *Meditations* and *Contemplations* cover reflections on a wide range of subjects, and he turns often to nature to point out ways in which God reveals something of Himself to man. He looks to nature, too, for object lessons in giving counsel to those seeking an intensely spiritual life.

DAVID BRAINERD (1718-1747)

David Brainerd's spiritual autobiography, *The Diary of David Brainerd,* is essentially a record of a human soul struggling to be at peace with God. Brainerd feared that he was among those who could not experience personal salvation, and he was rebellious toward the teaching that it should be "wholly at God's pleasure" to save him or condemn him. But as Brainerd thought about his rebellious spirit, he was persuaded that he deserved to be condemned. For several months he spent much time in prayer and fasting, often spending the entire day praying that God would open his eyes to experience personal salvation through Christ. One day when he was "walking in a dark, thick grove," Brainerd said he seemed to know "unspeakable glory" in his soul. Describing the experience, Brainerd said, ". . . it was a new apprehension or view that I had of God, such as I had never had before. . . . My soul was so captivated and delighted with the excellency, loveliness, greatness, and other perfections of God, that I was even swallowed up in Him. At least to that degree I had no thought at first, about my own salvation, and scarce reflected there was such a creature as I." From this time Brainerd came to realize that God alone must be exalted, and before one can know and experience salvation, he must come to God through Christ in the spirit of humility. Following Brainerd's new understanding of God's way of salvation, he emphasizes throughout the *Diary* the great need for Christians to work and pray for the salvation of people of all nations. The *Diary* allows one to see a remarkable Christian man unfold not only the longings and conflicts of his soul but also a vital personal faith manifesting itself in practice.

Although there is not a large quantity of religious works in the eighteenth century, the period produced several writings which were from a decidedly trinitarian perspective and which had as their controlling purpose the aiding of man in his quest of a godly life.

CHAPTER 4

The Nineteenth Century

LITERARY HISTORIANS often refer to three main trends in literature: Classicism, Romanticism and Realism. If the preceding century, with its stress on form and clarity, emphasized the first of these, certainly the nineteenth century saw the emergence of the latter two. To be sure, there is a blending of tendencies in all ages among writers, but certain characteristics are more pronounced in the writings of particular periods.

In the early nineteenth century a discernible revolt occurred against the rationalism and strict form of eighteenth century writers. Romantic idealism pervaded the philosophical world in the early part of the century, and in literature a Romantic revolt set in against the dominant tendencies of the eighteenth century. Rather than emphasizing order and lucidity, the Romanticists stressed freedom and imagination. They accorded a high place to the productions of the imagination and often rebelled against the Classical emphasis on the authority of reason. Individualism, personal experience, a love for humble folk and a zeal to remake the world were concerns of the Romanticists.

The Romanticists were also lovers of nature. The charm of the countryside, forests, seas and all out-of-doors captivated the Romantic writers. The eighteenth century Classical authors also spoke often of nature, but they were concerned with its geometric patterns and the power of man's reason to control it. The Romantic writers were interested in the loveliness and beauty of the sights and sounds of nature itself.

Among the early leaders of Romanticism were Jean Jacques Rousseau, Thomas Gray, Oliver Goldsmith, Robert Burns and Friedrich Schiller. As the movement grew out of its infancy, William Wordsworth and Samuel Taylor Coleridge became its great prophets in England. They were followed by a trio of outstanding English Romantic writers: John Keats, Percy Bysshe Shelley and George Gordon, Lord Byron. Although Romanticism had deep, long roots in England, it was not exclusively an English movement. In Germany, for example, it was championed by Heinrich Heine, and in France particularly by George Sand and Victor Hugo.

But as the years of the nineteenth century passed, the Romantic movement was supplanted by another literary tendency, perhaps best labeled Realism. Mass production, automatic and highly specialized industrial processes, revolutionized transportation, new social and economic doctrines, and new inroads of scientific thought provided man with a new environment.

Writers reacted in various ways to this new world. Some were convinced that they must look at life as it was—not as it should be or might be. They stressed objectivity toward life by documenting their stories with facts. This tendency pervaded many nineteenth century works under the label of Realism. The Realistic writers demonstrated an absorbing interest in psychological and social problems. They analyzed in detail the conflicts and struggles of individuals in overcoming the "deterministic" influences of their environment. Some Realists were guided by the evolutionary concept advanced by Darwin, interpreting man's behavior on the basis of his supposedly inherited bestial qualities. However, not all writers accepted the theory of evolution, and not all were willing to explain the intricacies of man solely on the bases of heredity and environment. Wrestling with doubt and despair occasioned by the theories of natural science, some poured out their struggles in their writings. Others turned to the Middle Ages in search of the noble, spiritual ideals which their world seemed to have lost.

Realism has many brilliant names in its camp, including Honoré de Balzac, Gustave Flaubert, Emile Zola, William Thackeray, Charles Dickens, George Meredith, Thomas Hardy and others. The nineteenth century is an age of many great changes and outstanding writers, including some who wrote from a God-oriented position.

JOHN HENRY NEWMAN (1801-1890)

John Henry Newman was born in London, the son of a banker. As a boy he was studious and devoted to reading. In 1816 he entered Trinity College, Oxford, and in 1822 was elected a fellow of Oriel College, Oxford. He became the curate of St. Clements,

Oxford, in 1824, and his great work in the field of religion began. During the following years he held various clerical positions in Oxford, and in 1831 he was appointed preacher to the university. About this time he was beginning to become dissatisfied with the English Church. Seeking spiritual and physical health, Newman took a cruise to Rome and returned from that city convinced that the religion practiced there was idolatrous. Still somewhat disquieted in spirit, on this return voyage Newman wrote the great hymn, "Lead, Kindly Light."

Upon his return to England Newman became a prominent figure in the Oxford Movement. Among the basic concerns of the Oxford Group was an attempt to revive the former beauty and simplicity of the English Church. In a series of pamphlets, *Tracts for the Times,* Newman castigated the liturgy (or lack of it) and the dogma of the Anglican Church. Step by step he moved closer to the Catholic Church, retracted the criticism he had previously leveled against it, and on October 9, 1845, became a Roman Catholic.

In 1846 Newman was ordained a priest. Accepting an invitation to become rector of the Catholic University at Dublin, he remained there four years. Because of lack of funds among the Irish and because of the Irish bishops' opposition to a university, Newman found himself rector of an institution that did not exist. Nevertheless, while at this post he delivered his famous lectures on *The Idea of a University.* He advocated such an enlightened theory that educators still consider many of his ideas basic to a philosophy of liberal arts education. As a treatise on liberal education it is outstanding. Perhaps the most troublesome event of Newman's life was his quarrel with Charles Kingsley, a clergyman, poet and novelist. In response to one of the pamphlets Kingsley wrote against him, Newman wrote his beautiful autobiography. In 1879 Pope Leo XII elevated Newman to the position of cardinal.

APOLOGIA PRO VITA SUA (1864)

The professed purpose of this autobiography was to refute a pamphlet written by Charles Kingsley. But rather than dealing extensively with Kingsley's attacks, Newman spent most of his time recounting the history of his own views. In doing this Newman wrote his spiritual autobiography.

The opening pages of the *Apologia* seem simply to lay down the earliest tendencies or biases of Newman's mind and the extent to which he was ready to accept or to reject these varying ideas. He mentions in rapid succession the somewhat mystical nature of his spirit and his view of skepticism. His reaction to the skepticism of Hume and Voltaire shows his own personal dislike for, and yet keen understanding of, doubt. In writing about the influence cf his colleagues in the Oxford Movement, he concentrates on his own state of mind rather than on their intellectual arguments.

Under the influence of a Calvinistic group, the studious young Newman took a stand as a believer in God in 1816, the same year he entered Oxford. Among the books he read at this time, and one that particularly impressed him, was William Law's *Serious Call to a Devout and Holy Life.* Through reading this work Newman became keenly aware of the constant warfare between the kingdom of God and the kingdom of darkness.

When Newman was made a fellow at Oriel College, where John Keble and Edward Pusey were also fellows, he became concerned that the English Church recover what he called the marks of the true church—holiness, apostolicity and catholicity. This concern led to the Oxford Movement. Newman and other members of the Oxford Group contended that their primary concern was to recover the basic fundamentals of the Anglican Church, a position they considered midway between Roman Catholicism and Protestantism. Newman held that Protestantism was erroneous in its teaching regarding the church and the sacraments, and in its disregard for apostolic succession. On the other hand, he believed just as emphatically that the Roman Church was in error in venerating saints and granting authoritative power to the Pope.

Newman was a leading contributor to a series of pamphlets called *Tracts for the Times,* and one of these, Tract 90, was the source of much turmoil in Anglican circles. This tract disclosed that some of the tenets of the Roman Church were not inconsistent with Anglican doctrine. When the tract appeared it caused such a stir that Newman's bishop pleaded with him to stop writing for the series.

Moving closer and closer to the Roman Church, Newman began to question whether the Anglican Church was not as schismatic as the Lutheran and Calvinistic groups. He admitted that the Anglican Church could claim apostolicity and holiness, but he doubted that it could claim catholicity. However, believing that his desire for a reunion between the churches of Rome and England would not be realized, and facing strong opposition from the Anglican leaders, Newman concluded that the Established Church would never again bear the marks of the Roman Church.

Newman was at this time serving as vicar of St. Mary's Church, Oxford. Since he privately believed that the English Church was not the true church, and yet held an important position within it, he proposed to resign as vicar of St. Mary's. And in 1843 Newman and a number of his followers retired to Littlemore, where they practically led a monastic life. But in 1845, when he became a Roman Catholic, he severed all connections with Oxford. The following year he was ordained a priest of the Roman Church.

Looking back after twenty years upon the controversy of the 1840's, Newman was convinced that he and his friends had fought their greatest battle against religious and political liberal thought. Fearful of the inroads of post-Kantian idealism, Newman stood against this movement of thought. Newman also expressed his alarm over the possibility of parliament becoming preoccupied with economic interests or dominated by a Whig hierarchy. He felt that his retirement from the Anglican Church had actively helped loosen liberal thought, for he said, "The men who had driven me from Oxford were distinctly the Liberals; it was they who opened the attack upon Tract 90, and it was they who would gain a second benefit, if I went on to retire from the Anglican Church." This is one of the few passages in the *Apologia* that indicates regret.

As a reader ponders Newman's spiritual autobiography he is impressed by the author's desire to know and experience deep, personal, inner satisfaction. The ideas advanced are not numerous, but his position is unmistakable. Newman believed that the Protestant emphasis upon subjective experience had neglected objective truth and produced many schisms. And as earlier stated, he strongly contended that since the English Church was schismatic in origin, it could never recover the holiness, apostolicity and catholicity of the Catholic Church. Newman further held that private judgment on spiritual matters was not a sufficient guide for a discerning Christian life. "The sacred text," says Newman, "was never intended to teach doctrine, but only to prove it, and that if we would learn doctrine, we must have recourse to the formularies of the Church." To Newman the authoritative church was a better guarantee against skepticism and atheism than private judgment.

Newman's autobiography contains a stronger objective note than some previously discussed. His restless mind, packed with wide and varied knowledge, examines issues with closest scrutiny. But threaded throughout the work is the author's intense search for a satisfying view of man and his relation to God—a Being which Newman says is "as certain to me as the certainty of my own existence."

NATHANIEL HAWTHORNE (1804-1864)

Nathaniel Hawthorne lived and wrote when Transcendental thought had made great inroads into American literature. The Transcendentalists placed much emphasis upon intuitive truth and knowledge transcending the reach of the senses. Nathaniel Hawthorne became the chief spokesman against this wave of thought. Satirizing the optimistic, utopian ideals of the Transcendental reformers, Hawthorne contended that their superficial ideals would come to nothing if man himself remained unregenerate. Embedded within Hawthorne's works are abundant evidences of the author's orientation toward Puritanism. In his short stories and novels one of his preponderant themes is the reality of sin (particularly hidden sin) and its consequences. Hawthorne also explores the dangers of the prevailing preoccupation with experimental science. In both his "Rappaccini's Daughter" and "Ethan Brand" he implicitly sets forth his view that the cultivation of science, to the exclusion of the cultivation of man *as* man, helps dehumanize man. In writing of Dr. Rappaccini in the former short story Hawthorne says, "His subjects are interesting to him only as subjects for some new experiment. He would sacrifice human life, his own among the rest, or whatever else was dearest to him, for the sake of adding so much as a grain of mustard seed to the great heap of his accumulated knowledge." Hawthorne was not opposed to science, but he was aware of certain tendencies in the mid-nineteenth century that could result if the scientist "lost his hold of the magnetic chain of humanity."

The Scarlet Letter is almost unanimously rated his best novel. Other works such as *The House of Seven Gables, The Blithedale Romance* and *The Marble Faun* also helped give Hawthorne a reputation as an outstanding American writer. There are weaknesses in his writings, but Hawthorne particularly knew how to handle the details of his works so that they released a single mood or impression.

THE CELESTIAL RAILROAD (1843)

This allegorical work is an adaptation of John Bunyan's *Pilgrim's Progress* and was written when Unitarian liberalism and Emersonian Transcendentalism were popular in the cultivated circles of New England society. Obviously satirizing these new liberal trends, Hawthorne makes it clear that he believes in the Puritan concepts of Christianity. He follows closely the various stages of Bunyan's allegory and on occasion appropriates the actual language of Bunyan.

But Hawthorne does not depict a lonely pilgrim clothed in rags, with his face turned from his own house, "a book in his hand" and "a burden upon his back" asking, "What must I do to be saved?" Instead he writes of the "pilgrims" riding along with the "burden of sin" deposited in a baggage car and the words of Mr. Smooth-it-Away pointing out the advantages of the celestial railroad over the old narrow footpaths of the uninformed pilgrims of former years. Large parties "of the first gentry and most respectable people of the neighborhood" were aboard the train and were as cheerful as if the pilgrimage were "merely a summer tour."

A bridge is now built over the famous "Slough of Despond" in Bunyan's *Pilgrim's Progress,* and Hawthorne has Mr. Smooth-it-Away describe it in telling satire: "You observe this convenient bridge. We obtained a sufficient foundation for it by throwing into the slough some editions of books of morality; volumes of French philosophy and German rationalism; tracts, sermons, essays of modern clergymen; extracts from Plato, Confucius, and various Hindu sages, together with a few ingenious commentaries upon texts of Scripture,—all of which by some scientific process, have been converted into a mass like granite."

Apollyon, the old enemy that Bunyan's Christian fought so fiercely in the Valley of Humiliation, is the chief engineer of the celestial railroad. Again in sharp satire Hawthorne says that "this shows the liberality of the age; this proves, if anything can, that all musty prejudices are in a fair way to be liberated. And how will Christian rejoice to hear of this happy transformation of his old antagonist!"

The Interpreter's House of *Pilgrim's Progress* is not one of the stations of the celestial railroad. However, the footpath still goes by the door "and the old gentleman now and then receives a call from some simple traveller and entertains him with fare as old-fashioned as himself." The new, comfortable railroad also rushes by the place where Christian's burden fell from his shoulders "at the sight of the cross."

On the other hand, Vanity Fair is still a prominent spot on the journey. But "there is no longer the want of harmony between the town's people and pilgrims, which impelled the former to such lamentably mistaken measures as the persecution of Christian and the fiery martyrdom of Faithful." The place is so charming that many affirm it to be the true and only heaven. And as Hawthorne relates, "the Christian Reader if he has had no accounts of the city later than Bunyan's time, will be surprised to hear that almost every street has its church, and that the reverend clergy are nowhere held in higher respect than at Vanity Fair." Among the clergy are the Rev. Mr. Shallow-Deep, the Rev. Mr. Stumble-at-Truth, the Rev. Mr. Clog-the-Spirit and the Rev. Dr. Wind-of-Doctrine. The whole atmosphere of Vanity Fair was so luring that not all seemed willing to pull themselves away for further pursuit of the Celestial City. However, amid the bustle of Vanity Fair there were two simple pilgrims, Mr. Stick-to-the-Right and Mr. Foot-it-to-Heaven, who repudiated the pleasures of this place. These pilgrims were following the footpath, and earlier on the journey Apollyon had puffed steam and smoke into their faces as he guided the celestial train.

Giant Despair is no longer one of the landmarks of the journey, but Mr. Flimsy-Faith repaired the castle once occupied by him and now "keeps an excellent house of entertainment. Throughout the journey the engineer Apollyon "screwed" many strange noises out of the whistle of the steam engine, but near the end of the journey, even though a "horrid clamor" was ringing in the passengers' ears, there came "an exulting strain, as if a thousand instruments of music . . . were struck in unison." The passengers soon ascertained the reason for such harmony: the two pilgrims who had taken the "narrow" footpath were entering the Celestial City. The celestial road had reached the end of its journey, but it could not "cross the river" and take its passengers safely to the other side of death.

Combined with the satire against Unitarianism and Transcendentalism is the attack upon any liberal theology which denies the presence of sin in a life and the need for a Saviour, and that which regards the journey of the Christian as pleasant and easy to travel.

EARTH'S HOLOCAUST (1844)

In "Earth's Holocaust," an allegory appearing in *Mosses From an Old Manse,* Hawthorne develops the same theme as in *The Celestial Railroad.* He tells of a "general bonfire" ignited by the citizens of the world in order to rid themselves of an overaccumulation of "worn-out trumpery." Into the flames are thrown all those things which perpetrate deceit and corruption, such as newspapers, titles of aristocracy, love letters and instruments of war and execution. Although the spirit of reform rages as intensely as the flames, Hawthorne shows, through as many satirical jabs as possible, that the bonfire is largely an excuse for a revival of trumpery, even in his hypothetical world come of age. New poets and philosophers propose to rid themselves of the weight of dead men's thoughts, while advocates of a new "natural" religion ruthlessly destroy the symbols of the old faith. Finally even the Holy Scriptures are tossed upon the blazing heap of falsehood (though they only shine the brighter for being purified of marginal notes). At this point the narrator of the story learns the allegory's essential lesson: Unless there is some fire that can purify man's heart, "that little, yet boundless, sphere wherein existed the original wrong of which the crime and misery of this outward world are merely types," the ashes of the blaze will merely "re-form" into the same (or perhaps even worse) sinful shapes. Though the thrust of "Earth's Holocaust" is typical of Hawthorne, it lacks the subtlety and skill of *The Celestial Railroad* and others of his greater works.

THE SCARLET LETTER (1850)

The Scarlet Letter is almost unanimously rated the best of Hawthorne's literary works and is a masterpiece of American literature. Choosing the subject of sin and its consequences as his main theme, Hawthorne shows the effect of one particular sin on the lives of four people: Hester Prynne, the Rev. Arthur Dimmesdale, Roger Chillingworth and little Pearl.

Hester Prynne, a beautiful young woman, was talked into marrying an elderly doctor and intellectual scientist, Roger Chillingworth. Later she came to Boston and fell in love with a promising young clergyman, Arthur Dimmesdale. They had a love affair, and Hester gave birth to a baby girl whom she called Pearl. A court of stern Puritan judges found Hester guilty of adultery. Condemned to wear on the breast of her dress the scarlet letter A, which stood for adultery, she had to stand in stocks before the meetinghouse so that her shame might be made public and serve as a warning to others.

The pillory scaffold on which Hester stood was located next to the balcony of the church where the bigoted officials of the Massachusetts Colony sat to watch her humiliation. The ministers of the town asked Hester to name the father of the child, who was really no less guilty than she. Even though the Rev. Arthur Dimmesdale implored her to confess as earnestly and eloquently as any minister, Hester still refused to name him as Pearl's father. After her period of public shame she was led back to prison in a state of physical and mental exhaustion. When a doctor was finally found, he turned out to be Roger Chillingworth. He also begged Hester to name the father of her child, but again she refused. Then Chillingworth warned her that he would not leave Boston but would stay there to practice medicine and spend the rest of his life in discovering the one who had dishonored him.

Meanwhile Dimmesdale, the father of Hester's baby, was paying a high price for his secret. His guilt constantly haunted and wore on him. Chillingworth, intimately acquainted with Arthur Dimmesdale both as his physician and parishioner, began to wonder whether his pastor might not be the father of Hester's child. Thus Chillingworth also began to prey upon the minister's mind in sinister ways.

Finally after seven long years Hester and Dimmesdale meet in the forest and she tells him who Chillingworth is and asks his forgiveness for withholding this information (she had promised Chillingworth that she would not divulge their relationship). Then Hester urges that she, Pearl and the minister leave for the Old World after Dimmesdale's "Election Day" sermon. Caught up in his old desires, the minister agrees to leave, but there is another development. The day after preaching his sermon, Dimmesdale, in the presence of the governor, magistrate and general populace, climbs the steps of the pillory where Hester stood in reproach seven years before and admits his guilt. Tearing the ministerial band from across his breast, he sinks to the platform and dies.

Within a year Chillingworth dies, leaving his property to Pearl, who has grown up into a rather capricious child. Hester leaves the colony for several years, but later returns and continues to wear the scarlet *A*, which becomes an emblem of mercy and kindness—an object of honor to those whose troubles she makes easier by her merciful and thoughtful acts.

Hester has been much admired, and justifiably. But Randall Stewart, scholar and critic of American literature, contends that she is not the protagonist, "and the tragedy of *The Scarlet Letter* is not her tragedy but Arthur's."[1] To Stewart, Dimmesdale's public confession "is one of the noblest climaxes of tragic literature. Poor, bedevilled Arthur Dimmesdale, the slave of passion and servant of the Lord, brilliant of intellect, eloquent of voice . . . the worst of hypocrites, and the prey of endless rationalizations and sophistries!"[2] The confession of Arthur Dimmesdale resolves the action of the novel. He saw and understood the gnawing internal conflict in his own life. He had to make a public confession, which "brought about a reconciliation with God and man; with, not least, little Pearl, from whom there had been a complete estrangement . . . Arthur saw . . . God's mercy: 'He is merciful,' he said; 'He hath proved His mercy . . . in my afflictions.' "[3] In the resolution of *The Scarlet Letter* and in "his profoundest character-creation . . . Hawthorne has employed the Christian thesis: 'Father, not my will, but thine be done.' "[4]

ROBERT BROWNING (1812-1889)

Some contend that Robert Browning is far more humanistic than Christian, and it is true that Browning was extremely interested in man. But one of Browning's central ideas is that because man is created in the image of God, he is of great significance. In Browning's religious poems one finds not only great art but some of the outstanding landmarks of nineteenth century religious thought. He is sometimes referred to as the "historian of the human soul."

Browning was born in Camberwell, at that time a suburb of London, where he lived for twenty-eight years. His father was gifted in the fine arts and literature, and both of the poet's parents were nonconformists. Although Browning did not attend either Oxford or Cambridge, he had rich educational opportunities in his parents' extensive library. He did attend London University for a few months, but his obvious education in art, history, music and the classics as well as his insatiable thirst for learning can be attributed almost entirely to the influence of his home.

Robert Browning's decidedly religious poems offer an intense psychological probing of the human soul as well as provocative comments upon the human condition. He attempts to understand the workings of men's minds and does not confine his comments to those of whom he approves. Browning is convinced that every person has a reason for thinking or acting as he does, the right to be heard and the prerogative to defend himself. Readers of Browning's dramatic monologues should try to keep in mind who is speaking, who is addressed and the purpose or motivation for speaking. Browning does not always agree with the particular acts he examines in his works: he simply wishes to understand the *why*. He is a psychological and philosophical poet as well as an artist.

"SAUL"

This extraordinary poem, based on the account of David's playing his harp before King Saul, is one of Browning's most beautiful works. It opens with a picture of Saul in the agony of spiritual conflict. Browning depicts an unforgettable picture of the tormented king:

> He stood as erect as that tent-prop, both arms
> stretched out wide
> On the great cross-support in the center, that
> goes to each side;
> He relaxed not a muscle, but hung there as,
> caught in his pangs

> And waiting his change, the king serpent all
> heavily hangs,
> Far away from his kind, in the pine, till deliver-
> ance come
> With the springtime—so agonized Saul, drear
> and stark, blind and dumb.

Young David took his harp and went, as bidden, to the tent of King Saul. He played songs that covered a great range of earthy life: songs of the animals, the music of human fellowship—the song of the reapers and the toilers, and the march of the honored dead. After that came the chant of marriage and the "world of our daily round of living in which we laugh with those who laugh and mourn with those who mourn; there is the world of worship in which 'Levites go up to the altar in glory enthroned.' "[5]

David's song celebrated the sheer joy of being alive, the significance of man's life, the never-failing providence of God, the gifts of God given to Saul and the many great deeds Saul had performed. Suddenly Saul relaxed from his agony, and his deep despair ceased. But even though he was awakened from his depression, he did not desire to live. So far David's songs had been only of the past and present, but then he began to sing of the future, the glorious prospects of Saul's race and the reward that God must have for his successor. The king began to live again. He touched the brow of David, and David's heart literally went out to him in such deep concern that he longed to give Saul a completely new life. But David realized that only God could give Saul what his soul needed; and in a beautiful outburst David sang a new song telling Saul of the Christ who loved him and opened the way to a new life for him. Browning states the thrust of the new song in this stanza:

> 'Tis the weakness in strength that I cry for! my
> flesh that I seek
> In the Godhead! I seek and I find it. O Saul, it
> shall be
> A Face like my face that receives thee; a Man
> like to me,
> Thou shalt love and be loved by, forever; a
> Hand like this hand
> Shall throw open the gates of new life to thee!
> See the Christ stand!

When David left Saul's tent and went home in the night, he was not alone, for clouds of angels who had heard David's new song hovered near him. As David worked among his sheep, the extraordinary events of the night continued to impress themselves upon his mind. Pondering whether it all could actually have happened, David heard the brooks and the trees underscore the actuality of the remarkable events as they said "with their obstinate, all but hushed voices— / 'E'en so, it is so!' " Browning's conclusions in "Saul" seem to be triumphantly Christian. Man may waste years, but God can redeem and rescue them from waste, for "what He has once made He can make anew."[6] Also pervading the poem is Browning's fundamental thought that though the perfection of the soul may begin on earth, it is ultimately achieved only in heaven.

"PARACELSUS"

"Paracelsus" underscores the Browning thesis that time is not long enough for man to learn the full revelation of God—he needs eternity. The author posits the questions of how truth can be found and the goal of life attained.

At first Paracelsus says that his questions can be answered through a knowledge of nature, history and man. Then he shifts to an opposite position and declares that he will learn only from within. Persuaded that knowledge is letting the truth out of the mind, not into it, Paracelsus asserts that his mind will pursue a trackless course alone.

Time goes on. Paracelsus knows success to some measure, but he is dying. As he faces death, he finds the solutions to his earlier questions. He discovers it is not through rational knowledge that man finds God, in fact a rational knowledge of God and life is not really what man strives to attain. Rather it is, in part, the power to live out his own knowledge as though it were a revelation from God to be made completely clear only after death. In brief, absolute knowledge is not gained through human ingenuity; it is a revelation of God, and time is not long enough for its complete communication. Eternity will reveal the entire revelation of God's divine plan.

"CHRISTMAS EVE"

In one respect this poem is a description of the events and a re-

flection of the thoughts one may have on Christmas Eve. But as
Browning so often does in his poems, he attempts to understand
the working of a man's mind. He describes the inquiring, intel-
lectually alert mind of a man as he sits in church listening to a
Christmas Eve sermon. Reflecting on the easily satisfied worshipers, fed on platitudes of truth at the Nonconformist chapel,
and the just-as-easily-satisfied worshipers, held breathless by the
mystery of the Mass or by the tinkling of the silver bell in the
great cathedral, the man finds both types far from his concept of
truth. Yet he must admit as the sermon ends that men's hearts are
blessed and Christ is made manifest.

"EASTER DAY"

Often considered a companion piece to "Christmas Eve,"
"Easter Day" describes another sacred day and considers another
deep issue. A believer and a nonbeliever argue over whether one
can believe in Christian revelation. But soon the dialogue turns
to the contrast frequently existing between *what* one believes and
how he lives out his belief. The nonbeliever, or the skeptic, contends that though faith in God is a necessity, scientifically it is an
uncertainty. Something of the intensity of the skeptic's concern
may be gathered from these lines:

> Could I believe once thoroughly,
> The rest were simple. What? Am I
> An idiot, do you think?—a beast?
> Prove to me, only that the least
> Command of God is God's indeed,
> And what injunction shall I need
> To pay obedience?

The believer responds that believing or knowing is not the big
issue. What a person does about what he knows often stands
in great contrast to his "belief." Questioning how a man living on
earth can shape his life, the man of faith is suddenly enveloped
in a tremendous vision. He is made to see that the earth is a
training ground for the soul, but a love for God includes a belief
in what God has done. Pleading with the man, the vision speaks
as the long poem closes:

> Now take love! Well betide
> Thy tardy conscience! Haste to take
> The show of love for the name's sake,
> Remembering every moment who,

> Beside creating thee unto
> These ends, and these for thee, was said
> To undergo death in thy stead
> In flesh like thine.

It is through genuine belief in the One who died "in flesh like thine" that man learns the secret of perceiving and doing the will of God. The wise man or the natural man is unable to erase the discrepancy between knowing and doing.

"A DEATH IN THE DESERT"

Browning explores what will happen to the "new" Christian faith in the ages to come. John, the beloved disciple of Christ, asks what will become of the Christian faith when men who have not known Him on earth as John did will begin to doubt what the disciple has seen and written. Looking back on those glorious days with the Master in Galilee and remembering His miracles and His words, John says: "It was so; so I heard and saw . . . / I saw, I heard, I knew." But many years have passed since those days in Galilee, and John is old, and men say, "Where is the promise of His coming?" As the years continue to pass, others will ask, "Was John at all, and did he say he saw?"

Browning reflects on how the awe and wonder of Christian revelation will be able to stand against the queries of man in time. As he muses, he declares that the Word of God was spoken for all time by Christ, and men living throughout the ages must live and grow by that truth. Men may have their times of doubt; John doubted, too, in the garden, but he came to see again. As one lives in wondrous faith, his whole being speaks aloud of the certainty of the Christian faith. The dead too speak of that certainty, and John still speaks, lying "as he lay once, breast to breast with God."

"RABBI BEN EZRA"

This poem is often considered the work that states most fully the philosophy implicit in all of Browning's poetry. In the mouth of Rabbi Ben Ezra, a medieval Jewish sage, Browning places some of his strongest convictions.

The poem depicts the mature individual and represents old age as the pinnacle of experience rather than a period of deterioration. In the opening stanza the rabbi speaks:

> Grow old along with me!
> The best is yet to be,
> The last of life, for which the first was made:
> Our times are in his hand
> Who saith, "A whole I planned,
> Youth shows but half; trust God: see all, nor be afraid."

In old age life is complete and as the rabbi looks back on the years he reflects on the meaning of life. He has no objections to youth's period of doubt. If one has doubts, it is a sign that he is not a brute. And if he has failed, it is a sign that he has striven, and the measure of man is what he aspired to be and could not attain. But just as it is the business of youth to experiment and question, it is the business of old age to pause and take stock before his final battle comes—death. It is good for youth to struggle, but it is wiser for age to rest, reflect and know with certainty. But he will "summon age / To grant youth's heritage." Browning reflects on the way God shapes human lives here on earth as a potter shapes a pitcher at the wheel:

> Ay, note that Potter's wheel,
> That metaphor! and feel
> Why time spins fast, why passive lies our clay,
> Thou, to whom fools propound,
> When the wine makes its round,
> "Since life fleets, all is change; The Past gone, seize today."

Man is as clay in the hands of God, the Potter, and the image of the potter's wheel shows why in youth everything "spins dizzily" and man is whirled in a dance of "plastic circumstance," for the Potter is shaping man. The poem concludes with a request:

> So, take and use thy work;
> Amend what flaws may lurk,
> What strain o' the stuff, what warpings past the aim!
> My times be in thy hand!
> Perfect the cup as planned!
> Let age approve of youth, and death complete the same!

Interwoven with the concerns for life is the certainty of immortality when the Master Himself will "pour" for man the "new wine" of immortal life and there will be no need for "earth's wheel."

"PROSPICE"

Written after the death of Mrs. Browning, "Prospice," which means "Look ahead," is a reflection of Browning's thoughts on death. He does not fear death but thinks of it as a battle and wants to watch it come:

> I was ever a fighter, so—one fight more,
> The best and the last!
> I would hate that death bandaged my eye and forebore
> And bade me creep past.

And as death comes, he writes, the tumult of the elements shall dwindle, and a peace and a light shall come. "Then . . . O thou soul of my soul! I shall clasp thee again, and with God be the rest!"

"CLEON" AND "EPISTLE OF KARSHISH"

"Cleon" and the "Epistle of Karshish" are two other Browning poems that are frequently classified among his religious poems. Battenhouse's position that they "interest us by their indirect approach to the study of the Christian faith, helping us to see how the early Christians were held in contempt as barbarous Jews or, simply, as queer people"[7] seems logical. And that each critic in the poems "is led to admit this essential truth of Christianity: that it effects a supernatural and spiritual regeneration in the life of the believer"[8] is another significant thought. The orientation of these poems may not appear to be as decidedly Christian as the works previously discussed. But the poet clearly implies that such great doctrines as the immortality of the soul and the divinity of Christ are rejected by doubting skeptics simply because they appear too good to be true. And he further implies that the skeptics simply want individuals to accept their doubting questions and to substitute them for great Christian truths.

Robert Browning's religious poetry implicitly reveals that the poet has examined some of the most vital concerns of the Christian: the doctrine of God, man's relation to God, the world and his fellowman, the significance of Christian revelation and the immortality of the soul.

CHRISTINA ROSSETTI (1830-1894)

Christina Rossetti, the sister of Dante Gabriel Rossetti, is considered one of the few outstanding women poets of England. A close study of her poetry suggests that she may not have received the depth and breadth of appreciation she deserves. She composed more than nine hundred poems with a strongly religious thrust, sixty of them in Italian. Some critics categorize her works as poems of fancy, religious exaltation and passion. In 1862 she published *Goblin Market* and took her place at once among the poets of merit of the nineteenth century. She also published several prose selections.

Perhaps some of the most intensely personal revelations of her inner strength and stability are found in her devotional prose work. Her devotional work, *The Face of the Deep,* is considered her greatest and "is almost worthy of a place beside Donne and Hooker or Lancelot Andrewes."[9] Another deeply personal prose work, *Time Flies: A Reading Diary,* appeared in 1885. Prose passages are alternated with poetry, and "the symbolic diary" contains meditations about the saints and martyrs, bits of personal philosophy and revealing autobiographical notes.

Christina Rossetti wrote numerous religious poems, many of them very brief. Some contain excellent lines; others fail to show that vitality of poetic art of which she is capable. Much of her religious poetry shows a longing to know God fully and a yearning to know the ecstatic bliss of heaven. The subject of death is another chief preoccupation of the poet.

A typical expression of Christina Rossetti's longing for God's protection is seen in a little work under the subtitle, "Lord, Save Us, We Perish." Here are the first few lines:

> O Lord, seek us, O Lord, find us
> In thy patient care;
> Be Thy love before, behind us,
> Round us, everywhere:
> Lest the god of this world blind us,
> Lest he speak us fair,
> Lest he forge a chain to bind us,
> Lest he bait a snare.

"Christ our All in All" is a series of short poems which she wrote over a period of years. Showing the unworthiness and weaknesses of human beings, Christina Rossetti clearly enunciates that Christ knew all about us, and yet He still wanted sinning creatures for

Himself because of His mysterious love. These two sections show
the essence of her insight into God's personal concern.

> Lord God of Hosts, most Holy and most High,
>   What made Thee tell Thy Name of Love to me?
> What made Thee live our life? What made Thee die?
>   "My love of thee."
>
> I pitched so low, Thou so exceeding high,
>   What was it made Thee stoop to look at me
> When flawless sons of God stood wondering by?
>   "My love of thee."

As she often does in her poetry, Christina Rossetti uses in this
poem flowers (particularly the rose and the lily) and animals
(especially the lamb) to release her intensely personal view that
Christ is " . . . our all in all."

"Not Yours But You" shows the writer's ability to manipulate
dialogue with rare dexterity. There is unusual strength, too, in
the simple uses of the monosyllables in the sestet which shows
a penetrating colloquy between Christ and the soul. Observe
these lines:

> "Give me thy youth."—I yield it to Thy rod,
>   As Thou didst yield Thy prime of youth for me—
> "Give me thy life"—I give it breath by breath;
>   As thou didst give Thy life so give I Thee.—
> "Give Me thy love."—So be it, my God, my God,
>   As Thou hast loved me even to bitter death.

Suffused by love for Christ, "The Three Enemies" is another
dialogue of the soul, this time with the world, the flesh and the
devil.

"A Better Resurrection" shows the barrenness of life and compares it with "a faded leaf," "a frozen thing" and "a broken bowl."
Yet there is a cry for a new quickening from God and a declared
assurance of a new vitality in resurrected life.

"A Christmas Carol" is a lovely lyric which tells of the God
of heaven coming into the world as a little baby and closes with
these familiar lines:

> What can I give Him,
> Poor as I am?
> If I were a shepherd
> I would bring a lamb,

> If I were a Wise Man
> I would do my part,—
> But what I can I give Him?
> Give my heart.

"The Heart Knoweth Its Own Bitterness" appears to be an indictment of human love, but it is also an injunction to individuals to "Have patience with His love / Who died below, who loves for thee above."

"Uphill" depicts life as a long journey uphill toward death. The poet will meet others who have preceded her, and there will be "for the night a resting place" and "beds for all who come."

"There Remaineth Therefore a Rest for the People of God" invites rest to "arrest my weary spirit," encourages the soul to "strain yet a little while to reach the goal," and promises that God "will sustain with everlasting strength" and ". . . thou, with John, / shalt lie upon My breast."

"Sleep at Sea" is often called Miss Rossetti's masterpiece. Rising to a majestic climax, the poem blends beautifully and realistically the supernatural and the moral. George Saintsbury called the poem one of the few great devotional poems in English. Christina Rossetti's religious poetry demonstrates the intensity of her devotion to God.

GERARD MANLEY HOPKINS (1844-1888)

Born in 1844 into a moderately High Church English family, Gerard Manley Hopkins remained a devoted British patriot until his death in 1888. As a student at Oxford Hopkins came under the influence of the aesthete Walter Pater and the Classicist Benjamin Jowett. Both of these men greatly influenced Hopkins. But before he left Oxford he came under the influence of another Oxford man, Cardinal Newman, who left Oxford in 1845 and began spearheading an English Catholic revival. Hopkins graduated in 1867, and the following year he became a Jesuit novice. Serving in several parishes in England and Scotland as a Jesuit priest, Hopkins also taught in a Jesuit school and later became professor of Greek at University College, Dublin.

Upon taking orders, Hopkins burned almost all of his poetry written in his younger years and did not write poetry again until 1875—and then at the suggestion of his superiors. His first production was his major long work and masterpiece, "The Wreck of the Deutschland." Hopkins' poems were read by only a small circle of friends during his lifetime, and they were not published until thirty years after his death. Hopkins was vividly aware of the hand of God in all things, and his poems reveal his sensitivity to the presence of God in all that concerns man and the world in which he lives.

"The Wreck of the Deutschland," a difficult but masterfully written poem, is built around accounts of an American-bound German ship which was wrecked on the Kentish coast in the winter of 1875. Among those drowning were five Franciscan nuns, exiles from religious persecution. Starting with the paradox of five nuns dying on the point of safety after they had just endured intense suffering because of their love for God, Hopkins goes on to examine some fundamental paradoxes within the Christian faith itself.

The first ten stanzas of the poem are devoted to praise of God and the comparison of His majesty and grandeur with the pettiness and littleness of man. Beginning with stanza eleven, the second section of the poem describes the sailing and destruction of the German ship with particular emphasis on the drowning of the five nuns. In stanza twenty-four Hopkins relates how comfortable he was on the night of the terrible wreck. Then the poet turns to some of the vexing problems that face any Christian thinker: Why do people suffer, or do some seem to be chosen to suffer while others escape suffering? Or, specifically, why were these five people who had already suffered chosen for destruction when safety seemed so near? In stanzas thirty and thirty-one Hopkins ponders the sacrifice and suffering of the Christ, and he recognizes that this is far more paradoxical than the suffering of the five nuns. The poem ends on a triumphant note of joy as Hopkins affirms the power of God which turns sacrifice into bliss and death into victory.

"God's Grandeur" is one of Hopkin's best-loved sonnets. Lamenting the ugliness brought on the earth by an industrialized age, Hopkins assures the reader that the grandeur of God is still inherent in nature and the Holy Ghost still hovers over the whole earth to bless it. Some of the imagery of this poem (as in all of Hopkins' poetry) is especially telling. He chose the image "shook foil" for the grandeur of God, and a series of images, "bleared . . . smeared . . . smudge . . . smell," for the stain and blight of industrialism.

"The Windhover" is another of Hopkins' familiar sonnets. As the poet observes the gyrations of the bird's soaring, he portrays his deep feeling for nature as a manifestation of God and His creative ingenuity.

"Pied Beauty" depicts Hopkins' love and appreciation for "dappled" things. "Glory be to God for dappled things" the poet begins and then illustrates the spotted or freckled things in nature. After minutely describing a number of "dappled things" in nature, he concludes his poem by contrasting changing things of nature with God whose "beauty is past change."

> All things counter, original, spare, strange
> Whatever is fickle, freckled (who knows how?)
> With swift, slow; sweet, sour; adazzle, dim;
> He fathers—forth whose beauty is past change:
> Praise him.

Hopkins' thought lies in the mainstream of the Christian tradition and it is inextricably interwoven in his style.

HENRYK SIENKIEWICZ (1846-1916)

Born May 5, 1846, Sienkiewicz received his schooling in Warsaw and graduated in 1870 from the philological faculty of the university there. His first novel, *Run to Waste,* appeared in 1872; his first short story, "An Old Retainer," in 1875. These were followed by other works of literary merit. In 1905 he was awarded the Nobel Prize for literature. During the early years of World War I he worked for the cause of Polish independence and helped bring relief for Polish war victims. He died at Vevey, Switzerland, November 15, 1916.

QUO VADIS (1895)

Vinicius, a young Roman patrician, came to Rome after duty in the colonies and visited his uncle, Petronius, an intimate friend of the Emperor Nero. Vinicius, who had fallen in love with Lygia, daughter of a foreign king, asked his uncle to aid him in getting Lygia as his concubine. Petronius took Vinicius' request to Nero, and immediately Lygia was ordered to the palace. Her foster parents sent Ursus as her servant.

At a rowdy party in the palace Vinicius attempted to make love to Lygia, but through the vigilance of Acte, who was a Christian and a former concubine of Nero, he was unsuccessful. Hearing that Lygia would be given over to Vinicius, Acte, with the help of Ursus, planned her escape.

Meanwhile the servants of Vinicius were on their way to Vinicius' house with Lygia where a great feast was to be held in honor of his success in procuring Lygia. But Lygia did not arrive, for on the way to his house a group of Christians attacked the servants of Vinicius, rescued Lygia, and took her outside the city walls to live with them.

When Vinicius heard of Lygia's escape he was wild with rage: "His face became blue, his eyes turned in his head, foam came out of his lips." Vinicius would have chosen to see the city sink in ruins rather than fail in his purpose. He and a crowd of servants searched for Lygia, and Petronius sent some of his men to guard the gates of the city, but all efforts to locate her were futile. Finally Chilo, a Greek sycophant, offered to find Lygia. Pretending to be a Christian, he discovered where the Christians met in secret. He and Vinicius, along with the giant Croton, followed Lygia, who was meeting with the Christians, to her house and attempted to take her away. A fight ensued in which Ursus killed Croton and Vinicius was injured. For several days Vinicius stayed with the Christians, who took care of him. Even Lygia aided in caring for him until she realized that she was falling in love with the Roman patrician, a courtier of Nero! And Lygia began to reason, too, that Vinicius had pursued her to make her his slave and mistress and had also told her that if she thought more of Christ than of him, he was ready to hate Christ. It seemed to her that "the very idea of any other love than the love of Christ was a sin against Him and against religion." But the charm which Vinicius exerted was attractive to Lygia, and her struggle intensified as she tried to decide whether to accept or reject his love. Finally she concluded she should stop coming near Vinicius, so she left him to the care of others.

While Vinicius recovered from his injury, he heard the Christians speaking at their meetings and was greatly impressed by their forgiving spirit, their good deeds and their philosophy of life. He heard their leader Peter tell of Christ and His miraculous power. He was ready both to honor and persecute Christ; he understood the greatness of His teaching, but he felt also "an irresistible repugnance" to it. He recognized that even should he possess Lygia, he would not possess her completely, for "he would have to share her with Christ." But for some reason Vinicius came to the place where he no longer desired to take Lygia by force. He kept up his contact with the Christians and later accepted their faith. Then Lygia agreed to marry him.

In the meantime Nero, the Roman emperor, had gone to Antium. There Tigellinus, Petronius' enemy and Nero's friend, suggested to Nero that he should burn Rome. Nero followed the proposed idea and the whole city became "one sea of flame." Not knowing that Lygia had left the city before the fire gained headway, Vinicius rushed from Antium to Rome in an attempt to save her, fearing all the while that he could not reach the city before it was turned into one "big heap of ashes." The masses were furious about the fire. Each person appeared to be suspicious of the other. The empress and the Jews at court persuaded Nero to blame the fire on the Christians. Chilo, the Greek who passed as a philosopher, knew where the Christians were hiding. Though they had already forgiven him for numerous crimes, he added another abominable deed to his evil doings and turned traitor. He gave Nero information about them and directed the guards to their hiding place. Horrible persecutions began, and the cry "Christians to the lions" rang through every part of the city. The prisons were overflowing with victims. Pity had died. Women were raped by the gladiators and fed to the starving lions. All Christians were sent into the arena for the entertainment of the mob. Some were crucified; others were burned alive.

Lygia, too, had been captured and imprisoned. From the moment she was seized, "the suffering of Vinicius surpassed human endurance. His soul was turned into one groan, his thoughts were confused. He ceased to understand what was happening; he ceased to understand why Christ, the Merciful, the Divine, did not come with aid to His adherents." Vinicius wanted to believe the whole ugly business just was not true, but "the roaring of the wild beasts informed him that it was a reality; the sound of the axes beneath which rose the arena told him it was a reality; the howling of the people and the overfilled prisons confirmed this." It became Lygia's turn to be led into the arena to entertain the frenzied crowds.

She was stripped and tied to the back of a bull. When the bull was sent charging into the arena, Ursus rushed in and locked his arms around the animal; and on Ursus' arms "the muscles came out so that the skin almost burst from their pressure" but he had stopped the bull and "the beast rolled on the earth with his neck twisted in death." The wild, astonished crowd clamored for the release of Ursus and Lygia, and Nero yielded to their demands.

Persecutions continued. The spirit exemplified by the tortured Christians was memorable yet incredible. When Glaucus, for instance, was burning alive, he looked down from the burning pillar and fastened his eyes on Chilo, the traitor. The eyes of Glaucus did not leave Chilo; at moments they were hidden by smoke, but when the breeze blew the smoke away, Chilo again saw those eyes fixed on him. At first sight of Glaucus Chilo "was twisted into a lump like a wounded snake." And as he continued to see and feel the gaze of Glaucus, he became more and more miserable. Finally Chilo stretched his arms upward and cried in a piercing voice, "Glaucus! in Christ's name! forgive me!" The head of the dying man moved slightly, and from the top of the mast was heard "a voice like a groan,—I forgive!" Moved by the forgiving spirit of the martyr, Chilo cried out in a loud voice that the Christians did not burn Rome, the guilty man was Nero. Fearing what would happen to him not only then, but also in eternity, Chilo was at the point of mental and physical collapse. But Paul of Tarsus met him, told him that God forgave the thief on the cross, a servant of Christ (Glaucus) forgave him in the hour of torture and grief, and Christ's mercy would now extend to him in forgiveness if he would ask for it. Chilo looked to God through Christ and asked for forgiveness of his many sins. Then Paul baptized Chilo. When the Greek returned home, he was seized by Nero's guards and led away to his death.

Lygia and Vinicius escaped to Sicily. Petronius and Eunice, a slave who loved him, bled to death in each other's arms after a physician—at Petronius' request—had opened the vein at the bend of their arms. Prior to this Nero had ordered the death of Petronius who, knowing this, invited a number of patricians to his home and read a biting attack against Nero.

Nero's subjects hated him, rebellion was in the air, and death was imminent for the emperor. With some of his slaves around him, he tried to take his own life by cutting his throat. Unable to finish the deed, he died as a slave plunged the knife into his throat while soldiers approached to arrest him.

Quo Vadis is a highly dramatic work of fiction. Tremendous tensions of conflict pervade the work, and a broad panoramic view of a dying Roman civilization forms the framework of the story. Christians—real, suffering, forgiving, live people—are among the inhabitants of this created world of fiction. Sienkiewicz has turned his historical re-creation and his vivid, dramatic conflict into a work which not only contains Christian themes but also a decidedly pro-Christian context.

Miscellaneous Religious Writers

Several religious writers of the nineteenth century produced tremendously influential works even though their writings were neither numerous, nor, in some cases, noted for their sustained artistic greatness.

JOHN KEBLE (1792-1866)

John Keble, author of a selection of poetry entitled *The Christian Year,* has sometimes been credited with doing more than any other man to bring about widespread quickening of religious life within the English Church during the nineteenth century. His poems are all lyrical religious meditations similar both in tone and form to those of the seventeenth century poet George Herbert. Without confining himself to the imagery of the Bible, he shows throughout his poems his intimacy with it and interweaves biblical imagery gracefully with that from other areas. As the title suggests, Keble's poems are written for each Sunday in the year. Several are included for special services such as Holy Communion, Holy Baptism and Confirmation.

Keble is not an artist of outstanding ability, but there are flashes of poetic power in his poems. He expressed the thoughts and sentiments of his day in the idiom of his times and transfused into them the Christian spirit.

GEORGE MACDONALD (1824-1905)

George MacDonald was a Scottish religious writer whose place in literature is difficult to characterize. G. K. Chesterton says of MacDonald, "He is in any case one of the kind that is most difficult to fix. He wrote nothing empty; but he wrote much that is rather too full, and of which the appreciation depends rather on a sympathy with the substance than on the first sight of the form."[10]

Hoxie Neale Fairchild, who refers to MacDonald as "the Scottish Seer," contends that "he deserves respectful treatment at our hands if only because one of the most distinguished present-day interpreters of orthodox Christianity has acknowledged a debt to him."[11] The reference is to C. S. Lewis who died in 1963. And Lewis himself says of MacDonald, "I have never concealed the fact that I regarded him as my master; indeed I fancy I have never written a book in which I did not quote from him."[12] Lewis admits that the texture of writing is as a whole undistinguished; but he just as readily contends that there are passages in MacDonald's works "where the wisdom and the holiness that are in him triumph over and even burn away the baser elements in his style."[13]

Perhaps MacDonald is one of those rare geniuses whose *person* is larger and greater than his works. At the same time various claims have been made for MacDonald as a poet, preacher, novelist, critic, mystic and writer of fantasy—"fantasy that hovers between the allegorical and the mythopoeic."[14]

Although MacDonald has probably written more significant single poems, *The Diary of an Old Soul* is undoubtedly his best example of sustained poetic power. *The Diary* is divided into twelve sections corresponding to the twelve months of the year. These sections contain a poem for each day of the month. Often showing the inner wrestlings and strife of "an old soul," MacDonald's *Diary* is flooded with the large, triumphant assurance of one who has pondered deeply the mysteries of the Christian faith.

Included here are two poems from his *Diary*. First is the opening poem in the January section; second is the last poem of the December division.

> Lord, what I once had done with youthful night,
> Had I been from the first true to the truth,
> Grant me, now old, to do—with better sight,
> And humbler heart, if not the brain of youth;
> So wilt thou, in thy gentleness and ruth,
> Lead back thy old soul, by the path of pain,
> Round to his best—young eyes and heart and brain.

> Go, my beloved children, live your life.
> Wounded, faint, bleeding, never yield the strife.
> Stunned, fallen—awake, arise and fight again.

> Before your victory stands, with shining train
> Of hopes not credible until they *are.*
> Beyond morass and mountain swells the star
> Of perfect love—the home of longing heart and brain.

In MacDonald's three volumes of *Unspoken Sermons*[15] he addresses himself cogently to the claims of God and the needs of man. One of the most succinct and perhaps most accurate views of MacDonald's preoccupying concerns in these volumes is captured in two statements: "He addresses the will: the demand for obedience, for 'something to be neither more nor less nor other than *done*' is incessant. Yet in that very voice of conscience every other faculty somehow speaks as well . . . and no man in modern times was perhaps more aware of the distinction between Law and the Gospel."[16]

MacDonald's novels indicate that he did not restrict his "preaching" to his *Unspoken Sermons,* for his novels often include prolonged religious discourses. But this is not to say that he did not possess the powerful imaginative ability to tell a fascinating story. *Phantastes* and *Lilith,* two of his best books, demonstrate an extraordinary, creative imagination. In a word, *Phantastes* is "a spiritual pilgrimage out of this world of impoverishing possessions into the fairy Kingdom of Heaven." And it brings home to the reader "in allusive burgeoning the celestial purpose of our daily existence."[17] Like *Phantastes, Lilith* is an allegory of two worlds— "each revealing truths of the other not ever dreamed of so long as only one is frequented. It both binds in one and unfolds the world of concrete Beauty and the realm of abstract Truth."[18]

George MacDonald is not a great theologian and probably not a great artist. Yet some of his works contain polished gems that cause the most severe critics to praise his artistic powers. Even in his faulty works one may find "something that disarms criticism and will come to feel a queer awkward charm in their very faults."[19]

HANNAH WHITALL SMITH (1832-1911)

Hannah Whitall Smith's most famous work is *The Christian's Secret of a Happy Life* (1870). There is no magic about her secret: she simply contends that the promises of God are to be accepted, believed and tested. Convinced that all of God's children feel instinctively that a life of inward rest and outward victory is their inalienable birthright, Hannah Whitall Smith outlines step by step the essentials of living this life. Beginning with the thesis that Scripture teaches that one can know this happy life, the author shows the responsibility of both God and man. Man's responsibility is to trust God, and God's responsibility is to do what He says He will do. However, man must trust and believe; he must not just *say* that he does. Although the great part of the book deals with man's responsibility, the author makes it clear that unless she believed with all her heart that God fulfilled His part, she would not have written one word of the book. The happy life to Hannah Whitall Smith is the life "hid with Christ in God." Recognizing the difficulties one often encounters when the Christian seeks to enter this life, she gives particular attention to the problems of consecration, faith, the will, guidance, doubts, failures and temptations. Her positive suggestions regarding how one may *know* that God guides a human life are among her most helpful thoughts. Contending that there are four means through which God reveals His will: the Scripture, providential circumstances, the convictions of our own higher judgment, and the inward impressions of the Holy Spirit on our minds, Hannah Whitall Smith declares that when those four harmonize, it is safe to say that God speaks. Though not a work of outstanding literary quality, *The Christian's Secret of a Happy Life* has spoken clearly to numerous individuals because it deals with duties, conflicts, needs and decisions common to man.

FRANCIS THOMPSON (1859-1907)

Francis Thompson was the son of a doctor and intended to enter the priesthood. His father urged him to study medicine, but he failed to complete his medical studies. For several years he lived in poverty, but in 1888 Wilfred Meynell, editor of a Catholic magazine, and his accomplished wife Alice, rescued Thompson, recognized his talent and encouraged him to write. He wrote three volumes of poems and one prose work.

Thompson's best-known poem is *The Hound of Heaven* which depicts in a stirring manner the paradox of man's flight from God and God's constant pursuit of man:

> I fled Him, down the nights and down the days;
> I fled Him, down the arches of the years;
> I fled Him, down the labyrinthine ways
> Of my own mind; and in the mist of tears
> I hid from Him, and under running laughter. . . .

No matter where the poet flees, "The Hound of Heaven" follows, but he concludes that he actually was seeking the very One from whom he was fleeing. In his use of elaborate conceit, paradox and imagery, Francis Thompson has sometimes been compared with the seventeenth century Catholic poet Richard Crashaw.

Other writers of the nineteenth century definitely revealed their concern over questions relating to the Christian faith. Some did not get beyond the questions and emerged as writers of doubt. Perhaps one of the most classic examples is the American author Emily Dickinson. She wrote numerous poems which show her preoccupation with Christian themes, but careful examination of her works seems to indicate that she wrote not as a poet of faith but as one unable to come to grips with her doubt. And Dostoevsky's *The Brothers Karamazov*, though unfortunately often read only as a psychological study of murder and parricide, confronts squarely the issue of man's choosing faith in Christ or refusing to choose and consequently living in slavish doubt. Though logic, history and the examples of others may be against a free choice, the choosing of what the "heart whispers," with no other guide than Christ, is the basis for a true faith. Refusing to choose and living in doubt lead to a negation which destroys.

The nineteenth century is a period of complex influences, but in the midst of the claims of Darwinian thought and the tenets of a naturalistic philosophy, some of the greatest authors of the era wrote from a God-oriented point of departure.

CHAPTER 5

The Twentieth Century

THE TWENTIETH CENTURY is an age marked by global conflict, social revolt and a growing reliance upon science and technology. Each of these three characteristics has brought with it an incalculable number of influences upon human thought and expression.

Literary artists during this century have been keenly aware of the kind of world in which man finds himself. The great novelists, poets, and dramatists have been deeply concerned about the social, economic, intellectual and political problems and about the hope and destiny of confused man. And in the words of the historian, Edward McNall Burns:

> . . . they were disillusioned by the brute facts of World War I and by the failure of the victory to fulfill its promises. Many were profoundly affected also . . . by the probings of the new psychology into the hidden secrets of the mind. Instead of being created by God just "a little lower than the angels," man seemed now to be a creature just a bit higher than the apes.[1]

A major depression and a second world war, combined with fearful dread of a third, have also had inestimable influence on writers of the twentieth century.

It is almost impossible to express in brief compass any adequate description of the literature that has already been written in the six and a half decades of the century. Obviously, too, the whole story cannot now be told. A look at some of the major writers will help point up certain directions, not only in twentieth century literature but also in the twentieth century world.

Shortly after the turn of the century there appeared a school of novelists and poets who formed the Catholic Revival movement around 1914. Some of the work of this group was not outstanding, but it did include at least four important authors: G. K. Chesterton, Evelyn Waugh, François Mauriac and Paul Claudel.

Perhaps the pervading moods of the 1920's were "disenchantment, cynicism, and preoccupation with the tragic fate of individuals."[2] The literary tone was set by the early novels of Ernest Hemingway and John Dos Passos. In *A Farewell to Arms* Hemingway vividly depicted the cruelty, futility and stupidity of war. In John Dos Passos' *1919* the portrayal of the prevailing bitterness and cynicism resulting from the failure of a guaranteed peace leaves an indelible impact upon the reader. Some of the early poetry of T. S. Eliot is an artistic commentary upon the banality and barrenness of the contemporary world, particularly as contrasted with the richness of traditional forces. "The Waste Land" presents a philosophic vision close to despair, and his poem "The Hollow Men" is saturated with the senselessness of modern man's empty, boring, synthetic existence.

Also in the 1920's Theodore Dreiser disclosed his rigidly naturalistic, deterministic attitude in the novel *An American Tragedy*. Thomas Mann gained widespread acclaim in his "psychological study of illusion and distortion of values by an artificial and decadent society"[3] in his *Magic Mountain*. Influenced by psychoanalysis, James Joyce in his greatest work, *Ulysses*, probed and analyzed the thoughts of a few central characters until the most intimate inner workings of man's mind were revealed.

The writers of the 1930's manifested a definite trend toward a preoccupation with societal problems. Many works were serious indictments of existing wrongs; others portrayed a hope for a new day; and others seemed simply to find wonder and beauty in whatever was around them.

John Steinbeck's *Grapes of Wrath* delineated the sorry plight of a poverty-stricken farm family fleeing from the "dust bowl" to the promising lands of California, only to find that these new lands were monopolized by corporations that exploited the working class. Pervading some of the writings of André Malraux is the thesis that man finds dignity, hope and meaning in life by struggling against prevailing injustices. His work *Man's Hope* showed the glory of man as he selflessly struggled against fascism in Spain. In Thomas Wolfe's novels *Of Time and the River* and *You Can't Go Home Again* there is keen awareness of the ugliness in the world and sharp indictment of many existing wrongs, but he still believes that one day the America he loves will discover the true meaning of her ideals.

The 1940's and 1950's demonstrate a continuation of many of the trends of the 1930's. There is a marked emphasis on atheistic existentialism particularly in the novels and plays of Jean Paul Sartre which reveal his impressions of man's meaninglessness in a world of nothingness. Saddled with the dreadful freedom to choose, man must make his own life even though, to Sartre, he is caught in an impasse of nothingness. Albert Camus reflects similar disillusionment and despair in his early works, but by 1957 in his novel, *The Fall,* there is at least a serious attempt to discover values by which man can live as man in a world described by some as "post-Christian."

But there is another obvious trend in the literature of this century. Titles of some of the best sellers indicate an interest in the religious field. *Peace of Mind, The Big Fisherman, The Greatest Story Ever Told* are among those. But more importantly, there are some distinguished men of letters whose works affirm an attitude and a belief that are definitely God-oriented. At the same time there are some interesting changes in the field of literary criticism. "Hardly a book of criticism appears without its chapter or two on the knotty problems of literature and belief,"[4] says Henry Zylstra. And he adds: "Such terms as Natural Goodness, Original Sin, the Fall of Man, Creation, Grace, the Pelagian Heresy, and the like, weave in and out of literary discussion as familiarly as they did in the older theological treatises."[5] Certainly one of the most encouraging aspects of the handling of these old familiar terms is that men who are artists as well as Christians are appropriating them. These men are not writing pamphlets or best sellers that are here today and gone tomorrow, but they are writing literature of high quality—the kind that has within it the seeds of permanence.

FRANÇOIS MAURIAC (1885——)

Considered among the great contemporary novelists, Mauriac is a skillful writer, sensitive to every nuance of situation and language. A powerful absorption with sin—or with a particular sin— often permeates Mauriac's novels, but there is also an intense longing for a release that will result in a settled peace. Two

works, decidedly religious in orientation, are *Viper's Tangle* and
A Woman of the Pharisees.

VIPER'S TANGLE (1932)

Viper's Tangle, considered by many to be François Mauriac's
finest work, is a searing portrayal of one man's bitter struggle
with loneliness, hatred and resentment, and of the all-but-invisible
action of divine grace in his life. Because of its distinctive form,
that of a journal or confessional, the novel has an immediacy
about it that involves the reader directly in the enormous suffering
of this tortured soul. And yet, through a gradual development
of character, one is able to share not only in the suffering of old
Louis, but in his redemption as well. A distinctive mark of the
Christian writer is the ability to see in fallen man a soul capable
of being redeemed by the incarnation and atonement of Christ.
Throughout the novel this hope of salvation glows even in the
darkest of hearts, revealing itself in the end to be part of that
dazzling blaze that is the Sun of Heaven.

The quote from Saint Theresa of Avila that prefaces *Viper's
Tangle*—"Lord, consider that we do not understand ourselves and
that we do not know what we would, and that we go infinitely
far astray from that which we desire"—presents a major theme
in the novel, that of the soul working at cross-purposes with itself
in its confused and misdirected quest for God. Old Louis, like
every other man, was born with the "impulse of humanity," the
impulse to love and to be loved in return. However, through a
variety of circumstances not always in his control, this natural
impulse was thwarted and misshapen. Ironically, the one respite
from loneliness offered by the love of Isa Fondaudege is the very
thing, once its true basis is discovered, that finally embitters Louis
and alienates him for the rest of his life. By channeling all his
devotion to the accumulation of wealth and the harboring of
resentment, he distorts the lives of those around him, scarring
his wife and family with the same grief that had disfigured his
own life.

Louis, possessed of an astounding clarity and honesty of mind,
is driven away from God by the shallow and hypocritical faith of
his wife, a woman cut from the same pharisaical mold as Brigitte
Pian in *Woman of the Pharisees* and perhaps serving as a model
for that later character: "That charity is synonymous with love

was something you had forgotten, if you ever knew it . . . there was not a single one of the Beatitudes which you did not spend your life in denying."

And yet the early love inspired by Isa gave Louis "an intense feeling, an almost physical certitude, that another world existed." Nor, even after that love turned in upon itself was Louis cut off from the human means of grace. There was his daughter, Marie, and Luc ("who was our little Marie come to life for me again"), and the young Abbe Ardouio with his life-giving words, "you are very good." Through each the secret of life and death had been whispered in Louis' ear. The Someone for whom his whole life longed had followed him under many guises: "Tirelessly I had sought to lose that key which some mysterious hand always gave back to me, at every turning point in my life." Finally, it is this same Someone—this invisible Hound of Heaven—that frees Louis from the swarm of vipers that had poisoned his life.

With the intervention of grace comes the realization that Louis' crime was not simply a hatred for his children, a desire for revenge and an insatiable love of money, but also his refusal to "look beyond those entangled vipers." Having spent his life "creating this old man dying of hatred," he realizes, before death, that he has been prisoner to passions that were not part of his deepest nature; that is, that he had lived his life for hate, when all he ever desired —his only hunger and thirst—was for a fathomless Love.

WOMAN OF THE PHARISEES (1941)

The same misdirected longing for love that manifests itself in the embittered old man of *Viper's Tangle* is seen again, no less forcefully, in Mauriac's later work, *Woman of the Pharisees*. Brigitte Pian, the novel's unforgettable protagonist, embodies that scrupulous Christian piety which, despite the "sounding brass" of good works, is all-but-untouched by love. With consummate skill in characterization, Mauriac probes deeply into this extraordinary woman, leaving no corner of her soul untouched, no aspect of her virtue unexamined.

Endowed with an uncanny ability to control the lives of those around her, Brigitte claims as her own "the pleasure which belongs, of right, to God alone; the pleasure of knowing to the full the destiny of another soul." But such knowledge without commensurate love can be highly destructive. And this is the effect of Brigitte upon her husband, her stepchildren, the Puybaraud couple and the Abbe Calou, all of whom have erred in her sight through unselfish devotion to another human being. In each case, her "spontaneous acts of mercy" were calculated to bring the un-witting sinner before the will of God; a will uncompromisingly "spiritual" in its abhorrence of the flesh; a will, in short, indis-tinguishable from that of Brigitte Pian.

Psychologically, *Woman of the Pharisees* traces the transforma-tion of Brigitte's totally self-centered piety ("she found each day ever stronger reasons for thanking the Creator that He had made her so admirable a person") into a Christian charity at once truly humble and spiritual—and never with a sacrifice of either realism or credibility. The turning point of the novel comes with the death of Octavia Puybaraud, a death for which Brigitte knows she is at least in part responsible. Her overwhelming sense of pride is wrenched from her, and she becomes, in Mauriac's striking words, "a woman lashed by the Furies of the New Dispensation." All the pharisaical gifts of judgment and condemnation that once placed her far above all others are summoned with the ruthless justice against herself. "I did not realize," says the novel's narrator, "the full horror of the torment they inflict upon themselves, those serv-ants of God who do not know the true nature of love."

But with Octavia's death comes not only an almost insufferable remorse, but the redeeming experience of forgiveness as well. As a result of her visits with the disgraced Abbe Calou, Brigitte ex-periences for the first time the "impulse of humanity," that is the impulse to love. She learns through the incarnate Christ to be truly human, to find a place for the passions in the lives of others, and through her "alarming and ridiculous" affair with Dr. Gellis, to make room for the emotions in her own life as well. Perhaps what she realizes above all else is that the same need for love can drag a man to hell or lead him to God, that Source of love toward which all men, blind or with the eyes of grace, struggle and strive.

This oneness of love, the inextricable bond between heaven and earth, is a preoccupation that unites *Woman of the Pharisees* with *Viper's Tangle*. Perhaps the thirst that leads old Louis to hatred and avarice or Brigitte Pian to legalism is the same as that which leads the saints, while on earth, to the shore of the "River of Life." As least such a possibility confronts the readers of Mauriac's novels and causes him to search behind the crusty façade of an old reprobate, or of a desperate sensualist, or, for that matter, of a woman of the Pharisees—and to see in that far country of the soul the intense longing for God, for union with that "Ocean of Love" across whose surface ripple our own infinitely inferior human affections.

T. S. ELIOT (1888-1965)

Born in 1888 in St. Louis, Missouri, Thomas Stearns Eliot belonged to a family with a distinguished ancestry, including a number of early educators and writers. He took his undergraduate degree at Harvard and then went to Paris to study at the Sorbonne. Returning to the States he continued his studies at Harvard but made another trip to Europe in 1914. Eliot married an Englishwoman in 1915 and took up residence in London. He returned to America periodically until the end of his life, but in 1927 he became a British citizen. In the same year he also became a member of the Anglican Church, and in the foreword to *For Lancelot Andrewes* (1928), Eliot declared himself to be "an Anglo-Catholic in religion, a classicist in literature, and a royalist in politics." After 1927 Eliot became increasingly concerned with Christianity in his poetry and drama. Although no more of a propagandist in his religious poetry than he was in such early poems as "The Waste Land" or "The Hollow Men," Eliot's poetic vision became one of fallen men as redeemed by Christ rather than the despairing vision of civilization as a wasteland. "Ever since giving out his 'Ash Wednesday' composed in the late twenties, he has, particularly in the poem sequence called *Four Quartets*, and in his successive dramas, borne in upon the modern man the inescapability of religious choice."[6] T. S. Eliot's poems clearly indicate his powerful spiritual perception.

"ASH WEDNESDAY"

"Ash Wednesday," which Randall Stewart calls "perhaps the chief Christian poem of our times,"[7] contains six sections. It begins with the speaker's lack of power to turn again to the world, largely because of doubt, and ends with a complete reversal. In the sixth section he can turn either to God or to the world, but although he *can* turn to the world, he now *wants* to turn to God. In the first section the poet is apathetic, dried up, having no hope to turn again to the world, and having lost his hope he abandons the struggle. But in the last section, although he does "not wish to wish" for the world, he *does,* and, as paradoxical as it may appear, this is a good thing. He is now alive; a will is renewed. But this "new" will is not to be separated from God. A will that does not "wish to wish" for the world but does is stronger toward God than a will so dried up and inactive that it does not "wish to wish" either for God or for the world. The vivid contrast between Parts I and II points up boldly the "turning" change of will which is the significant development of the six sections of the poem. With powerful and sometimes difficult imagery the poet describes stages of indifference, self-denial, moral vision, rising faith, dire need for divine grace and the renewed will. By the time the reader comes to the last stage of the poem, he recognizes that the sixth section is only an apparent paradox and is rather an underscoring of the weakness of the lethargy and emptiness of Part I.

"Ash Wednesday" supports well the thesis of Elizabeth Drew that the excellence of Eliot's own religious verse is in its unflinching truth to his moods of doubt as well as of faith. And "Ash Wednesday" as well as other poems indicate that his acceptance of the Christian faith "was no easy leap . . . it was 'the time of tension between dying and birth.' "[8]

"JOURNEY OF THE MAGI"

"Journey of the Magi" depicts the tension between "dying and birth." One of the magi recounts the experiences on the journey to the Christ long after the journey is over and ponders the consequences. The clarity of the external details of the journey combine in this poem with the perplexity of its spiritual significance.

The poem begins with a quotation from one of the sermons of the seventeenth century bishop Lancelot Andrews:

> A cold coming we had of it,
> Just the worst time of the year
> For a journey, and such a long journey:
> The ways deep and the weather sharp,
> The very dead of winter.

Eliot then moves the poem through a series of obstacles provided by both nature and man to make "such a long journey" more difficult to endure. Enumerating precisely one obstacle after the other, the poet interrupts the cold calculations with only one emotion, the regret caused by recalling the life lived before the beginning of the long journey.

But the next paragraph opens with a ray of hope. There is evidence of life and growth in the "temperate valley," the smell of "vegetation," the "running stream" and the "vine-leaves." And in this section, the reader is aware of far more than the signs of life. The signs of a "death" which brings "Birth" are evident in the "three trees on a low sky" and "six hands dicing for pieces of silver." These hints of the crucifixion lead the reader into the last movement of the poem.

The speaker remembers in the last paragraph that the physical journey "was a long time ago" and he says he "would do it again." Then he concludes:

> This set down
> This: were we led all that way for
> Birth or Death? There was a birth, certainly,
> We had evidence and no doubt. I had seen birth and death.
> But had thought they were different; this Birth was
> Hard and bitter agony for us, like Death, our death.
> We returned to our places, these Kingdoms,
> But no longer at ease here, in the old dispensation,
> With an alien people clutching their gods.
> I should be glad of another death.

Pondering the consequences of that journey of the magi, the speaker recounts that the magi went to a birth, but *their* rebirth, because of a "Death," was a death to their old life. And he would make that journey again even though he now knows the hardships of being an alien among people "clutching their gods."

FOUR QUARTETS (1943)

Eliot's most complete vision of the Christian experience is probably seen in his long poem, *Four Quartets*, which beautifully integrates such themes as contemplation and action, and time and eternity. Consisting of four symmetrical meditations, the poem depicts the various aspects of the Christian faith, or more particularly the journey to that faith. Each quartet is named for a geographical location and identified with one of the four medieval medicines.

In "Burnt Norton"—named after a Gloucestershire manor—

Eliot struggles with the way the "time" of the past and "time" of the future force a "dark night" upon the soul. Reducing the past and the future into the present, a semblance of eternity, the poet reveals the need for man to know the timeless in time, to conquer the limitations of time and to see all things in light of eternity.

The second section of the poem, "East Coker," named for a small village in Somersetshire, continues the struggle over the relation of time to things, but begins to reveal how existence may have meaning. "In order to possess what you do not possess / You must go by the way of dispossession," says Eliot. But Eliot knows that self-abnegation is not sufficient in itself. Diseased man and a diseased world need an objective cure, and the poet makes clear that the ultimate cure depends upon Christ—the wounded surgeon. Even though health is found in the redeeming Christ, Eliot does not let the reader forget that there are eternal paradoxes in the Christian life.

The "Dry Salvages"—rocks off the New England coast—the third section of the poem, deals with many of these paradoxes. For example, there are moments of great illumination and ecstatic insight, as well as moments of everyday Christian living. But these high moments and the daily living in "prayer, observance, discipline, thought, and action" are fused in the incarnation. For Eliot says, "Here the impossible union / Of spheres of existence is actual / Here the past and future / Are conquered and reconciled, and this occurs because God stepped into time."

The fullness of reconciliation between God and man is sharpened in the last of the *Four Quartets*, "Little Gidding"—which was the seventeenth century Anglican community. Eliot through his potent images releases the view that the change, suffering and strife of earth are all transitory. Death is not the end; it is a door that marks the beginning. It is an entrance to true life which follows the purification by divine fire, and then "all shall be well and / All manner of things shall be well. . . ." To Eliot change, sin, suffering, or even despair are not the last words. They belong to a fallen world and come to an "end" for man when he is ushered into his new "beginning."

Eliot's preoccupation with Christian concepts may also be studied in his important dramas, of which *Murder in the Cathedral* is the most significant.

MURDER IN THE CATHEDRAL (1935)

Murder in the Cathedral is not simply a dramatization of the death of Thomas à Becket nor is it a "historical drama" in the usual sense of that term. By subordinating all the issues surrounding Thomas' death to the central one—that of martyrdom and its consequences—Eliot creates a spiritual pageant close to the medieval mystery plays and moral interludes. The Four Tempters of Part I, for instance, have no historical actuality nor are they naturalistically conceived characters. But as symbolic representation of those forces which waged war within Thomas and as striking prefigurement of the Knights of Part II, the inclusion of the Tempters is a dramatic *tour de force,* and to be sure, a symbolic effect that is in keeping with the overall tone of the play.

While *Murder in the Cathedral* is poetic in its language and ritual, its movement and whole dramatic and spiritual thrust is liturgical. In fact, one might quite easily say that the play is really more about the response of the people of God to the sacrifice of their pastor than it is about the archbishop himself. Thomas has purged his will before the end of Part I, and the action of the drama, rather than tracing any real character development, shows the growing consciousness of the women of Canterbury, both in their own implication in the archbishop's death and in the saving awareness of God's transcendence which that death brought to them.

But such knowledge comes gradually and only with a terrifying passage through the dark night of alienation. The chorus, "a type of the common man," does not at first understand that "acting is suffering, And suffering action." It remains for Thomas—a type of Christ, who like his Lord endures temptation and is strengthened by it—to bring his people to salvation. Thus Becket is tested, slain and exalted, not for his own sins but for those of other men. And though at the outset the chorus senses that "a new terror has soiled us, which none can avert, none avoid," they cannot make a full acknowledgment of their sin until Thomas has overcome the "Lords of Hell" and nurtured the church with his blood.

At the end of the play, after the knights have delivered their shoddy apologia in the name of "disinterest" (a travesty on the perfection of Thomas' emptied will) the chorus arrives at a full knowledge of what has transpired. They rejoice and mourn in one song, praising God all the while for raising up another saint in Canterbury. In contrast to their previous state—"living and partly living," terrified of "a disturbance of the quiet seasons" and of the brutality of "ruinous spring"—the women at last experience the fullness and reconciliation promised by their pastor. The seasonal imagery which dominates the play throughout no longer reflects the destruction of the natural order but rather its redemption.

And so with Thomas' sacrifice recalling that other unspeakable death, the women of Canterbury realize at last that the blood of the martyrs and saints is that "which forever renews the earth / Though it is forever denied." Seeing that vision of grace—"the darkness declares the glory of the light"—they break through to the still point of action and suffering to that absolute harmony where all wills, even those which deny, are united to the love which governs the universe and binds all of life to itself.

The Cocktail Party (1949), though not of the literary caliber of *Murder in the Cathedral*, articulates the emptiness and aloneness of modern man, but at the same time shows man's need for atonement and reconciliation.

C. S. Lewis (1898-1963)

C. S. Lewis was born in Belfast, Ireland, in 1898. Trained at Oxford, he was elected a fellow of Magdalen College, Oxford, in 1925 and continued his academic career at Magdalen until 1955, when he became lecturer of Medieval and Renaissance Literature at Cambridge University. He held the latter position until a short time before his death in 1963.

The road from atheism to theism is long and filled with transitions for C. S. Lewis, and he gives his own brilliant account of this route in his *Surprised by Joy*. Near the end of the book, Lewis describes an unforgettable picture of himself as he admits that God is God:

> You must picture me alone in that room in Magdalen, night after night, feeling, whenever my mind lifted even for a second from my work, the steady, unrelenting approach of Him whom I so earnestly desired not to meet . . . . In the Trinity Term of 1929 I gave in, and admitted that God was God, and knelt and prayed: perhaps, that night, the most dejected and reluctant convert in all England.

Lewis admits that this step was conversion to theism only. His deep belief in Christianity comes later. *The Pilgrim's Regress*, an allegory published in 1933, gives broadened understanding into what "might well be called the further spiritual adventures of C. S. Lewis."[9] Visualizing man in a search for meaning in life, Lewis shows him progressing from realism to idealism, to pantheism, to theism, and finally to Christianity. Though this journey may not be every man's journey from the beginning of his quest to ultimate satisfaction, Lewis reveals that lasting answers to man's perplexing questions lie in the acceptance of God's love personified in Jesus Christ. When man embraces Christianity he can then integrate morality, virtue, or any of those qualities which he initially believed to be ultimate answers, into a unified philosophy based upon love and faith in Christ.[10]

A volume on the sixteenth century in the *Oxford History of English Literature* and *The Allegory of Love* are the two most specialized, scholarly works of Lewis. His other writings, in addition to *Surprised by Joy*, include a variety of fiction, nonfiction and poems. Perhaps the most widely known of Lewis' works is *The Screwtape Letters*, typical of his grace, wit, imagination and powerful thought. This volume is singled out for special study from among Lewis' works.

THE SCREWTAPE LETTERS (1942)

The literary form of *The Screwtape Letters* is an imaginary correspondence between Screwtape, a devil in hell, and Wormwood, a devil on earth, whom he is instructing in ways and means of luring a particular human being from the path of virtue to the empty pleasures of vice. Wormwood is counseled not to let his patient acquire "the fatal habit of attending to universal issues and withdrawing his attention from the stream of immediate sense experiences. Your business is to fix his attention on the stream. Teach him to call it 'real life' and don't let him ask what he means by 'real.' "

Screwtape's basic instruction to Wormwood embraces two areas: the first is concerned with advice on how to keep his subject from becoming a Christian; the second is filled with counsel on how to destroy faith if the one entrusted to his "care" should become a Christian.

Centuries ago, Screwtape contends, argumentation could have

been successfully used to keep a thinking, intelligent person from accepting Christianity, for in the past individuals knew when a proposition was proved and when it was not. Today the picture is very different. Contemporary man can be at home in varying philosophies regardless of their incompatibility, for the question of whether a proposition or a philosophy is true or not true, proved or unproved, is not really important. What *is* important is to get the individual in the habit of using particular labels or terms such as old-fashioned or contemporary, academic or practical, to describe a given doctrine or philosophy. Jargon and unfounded attitudes, not genuine argument, can be a successful means of keeping one from becoming a Christian. Despite the advice from the more experienced devil, Wormwood is unsuccessful in keeping his subject from becoming a Christian.

But Screwtape has a second course of instruction. There must be a plan for destroying faith and belief, and one of the best places to start is with the visible church. The new believer is encouraged to criticize the liturgy, to point an accusing finger at hypocritical church members, and to start looking around for the church that suits him. He may find a preacher with designs to humiliate or to confuse his hearers. Or he may find one who is really not concerned about the tenets of the faith or the use of liturgy.

Instruction on the prayer life of the new Christian is most essential. Get the subject concerned over how he feels as he prays, and cause him to believe that the real value of his prayer life is measured in terms of the amount of feeling he is able to attain.

Times of war may create the atmosphere in which faith can be destroyed. Because the contemporary world is prone to band together during times of crises brought on by extreme positions, one should capitalize on this tendency. When wars are raging, it does not matter whether the subject entrusted to Wormwood is a patriot or a conscientious objector. But it is important to get him to adopt an extreme position and to make it a part of his religion. The next step is that it becomes the whole of his religion.

Wormwood is strongly advised to watch the spiritual life of the new Christian. When the Christian faces times of depression, he should be led to believe that this is not normal. From there he may simply be satisfied to live the Christian life with little ardor, or he may conclude that he really never did believe. What he took to be faith was no more than an exciting, adolescent stage in his development.

Every effort must be made to bring the Christian into the company of pseudointellectuals who question everything. This is a sure way of appealing to his social and intellectual pride and of leading him into the role of the skeptic and the self-satisfied. He must never be allowed to know the deep joy of the Christian life. Going through external practices of a Christian is quite all right as long as he fails to probe into inner significance of external habits. He may even demonstrate humility, but when he does, Wormwood must make sure that his subject recognizes and becomes proud of his own humility.

The new Christian must also be encouraged to be intemperate in the area of food and sex. Adopting a cynical attitude toward sex and marriage is the ideal for Wormwood's patient.

Making Christianity simply a means to an end is another way of distracting the Christian from real matters of faith. Combine it with some good cause, and the attention will be taken from Christianity and focused on the cause. Consequently, the cause can become a substitute for Christ.

Lewis makes poignantly clear that the plans of Screwtape and Wormwood are hampered by the "Enemy," God; and God loves human beings. While the author buoyantly satirizes many of the pretensions and practices of both the believer and nonbeliever of the twentieth century, he affirms that the love and mercy of God are sufficient to overcome the program of Screwtape and Wormwood.

Edmund Fuller calls C. S. Lewis "an important voice in the great debate: What is the reality of our being and our environment? The doctrine of creation . . . and the doctrine of man (as . . . responsible, guilty, redeemable creatures of God) are high in his concern."[11] This position Fuller further cites as the cause of the extremes of acceptance or rejection which Lewis arouses in his readers. Both within and without Christian circles he has his enemies. But to scores of readers C. S. Lewis is "one of the most distinguished present-day interpreters of Christianity."

W. H. AUDEN (1907——)

Wystan Hugh Auden, the son of a distinguished physician of broad scientific interest, was educated at Christ Church, Oxford.

Both of Auden's grandfathers and four of his uncles were Church of England clergymen, and the atmosphere of his home was devoutly Anglo-Catholic.

Shortly after Auden's graduation from Oxford he became associated with a circle of young poets in London, and partially due to their influence, began to produce poetry. His first book-length collection appeared in 1930.

Auden is the author of numerous poems and several dramas, and his works reflect a preoccupation with a variety of concerns. *For the Time Being* is "the fullest and most balanced expression of Auden's religious attitudes; the ideas and dominant images that have been seen partially and transitionally in other poems here may be seen in their final place as part of an ordered whole."[12] Because of the inclusive nature of *For the Time Being* it will serve as the classic example of Auden's religious writings.

FOR THE TIME BEING (1941/42)

"A Christmas Oratorio" is the subtitle of *For the Time Being*. The work follows the oratorio form except that musical setting is not essential. Monroe Spears says that the oratorio differs from the plays "in presenting a story both historical and thoroughly familiar, so that the traditional Christmas pageant or tableau can be suggested, as well as the miracle play, and the lighter elements of popular song and contemporary language can more effectively surprise the reader who expects a wholly solemn . . . work."[13]

"A Christmas Oratorio" follows the episodes of the nativity narratives in the Gospels, and at the same time the author is able to register the intellectual and spiritual predicament of modern man.

"Advent," the first section, discloses the exhaustion of the ancient world on the eve of the birth of Christ. Parallel to this historical situation run the themes of man's predicament without Christ, and as the title suggests, the annual church season of preparation for Christmas. The opening chorus suggests exhaustion and weariness. Two times the semichorus interrupts to point up the loss of hope of a secular savior. Mighty Hercules of the ancient Greeks is not able to revive the dying empire, for he, too, is lost. The chorus continues to utter its weary lamentations, and following an interruption by the narrator, the chorus despairingly chants, "Alone, alone, about a dreadful wood / Of conscious evil runs a lost mankind" and concludes, "We who must die demand a miracle," because "Nothing can save us that is possible." The "Advent" section closes with a recitative sharpening the paradoxical nature of Christian truth and a chorus pulling clearly into focus man's condition and the temptations peculiar to him.

The second section, "Annunciation," begins with the four faculties of man—intuition, feeling, sensation and thought. Sundered from each other since the fall of man, the four faculties are represented in their separate chaotic self-assertion as false guides. These faculties are the "Ambiguous causes / of all temptation." In a series of beautiful lyrics, Auden tells of the annunciation itself.

"The Temptation of Joseph" is the third section and can be easily misinterpreted. Auden realistically depicts the attempt of Joseph to have faith in spite of appearances. Joseph asked for "one / Important and elegant proof / That what my Love had done / was really at your will / and that your will is Love." Gabriel replies, "No, you must believe; / Be silent and sit still." Following rather light comments by the narrator on the relation between the sexes, the close of the third section comes with the semichorus asking Mary and Joseph to pray for various sinners, the first kind being those romantic lovers who believe "Simultaneous passions make / one eternal chastity." They are also invoked to pray for the unborn babies, who are already guilty of original sin, and finally, for the bourgeoisie with their "indolent fidelity."

The fourth section, "The Summons," contrasts human wisdom with Christian revelation. The inadequacy of classical philosophy and ancient political thought are sharply drawn. The wise men realize that they are "three old sinners" and that they have placed their trust in the wrong source. The Star of the Nativity stresses the need for faith and explains to the wise men "I am that star most dreaded by the wise / For they are drawn against their will to me." But the wise men are told that they must live by faith even as they endure hardships.

There comes next the Fugal-chorus in praise of Caesar's proclamation. Great tribute is paid to the Seven Kingdoms conquered by Caesar, which are tremendous achievements in the civilization of which man boasts. These Seven Kingdoms are: Abstract Idea, which embraces the disciplines within the humanities; Natural Cause, apparently the natural sciences; Infinite Number, obviously mathematics; Credit Exchange, the monetary system; Inorganic Giants, the huge machines; Organic Dwarfs, probably drugs;

finally, Popular Soul, techniques of mass propaganda. The acclaim over the achievement of man is followed by another boast
contained in the narrator's news broadcast which contends "Our
great Empire shall be secure for a thousand years." Auden follows with the words:

> In our bath, or the subway, or the middle of the night,
> We know very well we are not unlucky but evil,
> That the dream of a Perfect State of No State at all,
> To which we fly for refuge, is a part of our punishment.

And he further asserts "that the Kingdom of Heaven may come,
not in our present / And not in our future, but in the Fullness of
Time."

"The Vision of the Shepherds" presents the shepherds as poor
people but certainly with human dignity. The Shepherds identify
the characteristic common to all men: ". . . each of us is waiting"
for the same news. The Chorus of Angels announces the "ingres-
sion of Love" and that the "Authoritarian / Constraint is replaced
/ By his Covenant. . . ."

"At the Manger" is a scene of a lullaby sung by Mary in which
she ponders the way motherly care can bring sorrow to the Christ
Child. To the manger the wise men come with their gifts, but
rather than the traditional gifts, these bring their bodies and
minds to offer to Christ. Emphasis is placed upon the power and
seriousness of love, and in the acclamation of the wise men at the
manger one catches something of the significance of incarnate
love: "O Living Love replacing phantasy / O Joy of life revealed
in Love's creation."

In contrast to the stress of love in "At the Manger," the next
section, "The Meditation of Simeon," reflects on the philosophical
meaning of the incarnation. There is a prevailing view that
Simeon's meditation is probably the clearest short exposition of
W. H. Auden's religious position. The meditation is in prose, and
this is the first time prose is used in the oratorio. One-line allitera-
tive comments by the chorus are interspersed with the prose statements and these give a grippingly emotional power to the intellectual exposition.

Explaining first of all that before the incarnation could occur
man had to understand the nature of the fall, the nature of sin,
and the failure of any other remedy, Simeon declares: "The Word

could not be made Flesh until man had reached a state of absolute contradiction between clarity and despair in which they would have no choice but either to accept absolutely or to reject absolutely." And "that which hitherto we could only passively fear as the incomprehensible I AM, henceforth we may actively love with comprehension that THOU ART." Simeon then clarifies what this great truth means for man, for time and for history, but undoubtedly the greatest significance is what it means for truth itself. "Because in Him the Word is united to the Flesh without loss of perfection, Reason is redeemed from incestuous fixation on her own Logic, for the One and the Many are simultaneously revealed as real." Simeon thus declares the *oneness* of truth. And "the possibilities of real knowledge are as many as are the creatures in the very real and most exciting universe that God creates with and for His love."

The only other prose speech is in the next section, "The Massacre of the Innocents," and it is given by Herod who is both the historical king and the liberal of the late 1930's. Herod is troubled that his program to override superstition may be in serious peril because of the new, sudden invasion of the irrational associated with Simeon's "reasoning." As Herod thinks on the probable consequences for his plans and kingdom, he decides that his only alternative is to call out the military, and the soldiers ironically reveal the end of Herod's decision—to massacre the innocents.

The final section, "The Flight into Egypt," shows Joseph and Mary facing temptations from Voices of the Desert as they journey through "the looking-glass" which is usually taken to mean the journey of faith. The Voices of the Desert are apparently the temptations of the modern world in particular. Wild, nonsensical songs are the techniques of these voices. Joseph and Mary clearly see insecurity as the plight of modern man: "Safe in Egypt we shall sigh / For lost insecurity." But the final section focuses through the narrator's speech especially upon the way Christmas is commemorated by modern man in contrast to its deep, spiritual significance. And this practice of modern man seems to be perennial, for "Once again / As in previous years we have seen the actual Vision and failed / To do more than entertain it as an agreeable / Possibility, once again we have sent Him away. . . ."

"The Christmas Oratorio" has had a varied reception. Some criticize it for its obscurity; others feel that too many realistic details have crowded in upon a serious, solemn subject. Some critics praise its uniqueness; others show its similarities to Eliot's *Four Quartets*. But there is great range in the scope of "The Christmas Oratorio" which is implicitly released in the formal variety of Auden's verse and prose.

OTHER RELIGIOUS WRITERS

There are other playwrights of the twentieth century whose works are of quality and deserve a wider reading audience. Among these are Charles Williams and Dorothy Sayers. Williams is perhaps best known in the United States as a novelist. Although his novels are difficult and contain numerous esoteric ideas and allusions, his pages teem with passages of extraordinary prose. Williams' *War in Heaven*, for example, which presents the terrible conflict between good and evil in the universe, vividly reveals fineness in character drawing and depth of psychological understanding. Williams' play, *The Rite of the Passion*, written for a Good Friday service in 1929, contains a number of the ideas that appear in his later plays. Divided into four parts, the play deals with the annunciation, the betrayals, the crucifixion and the resurrection of Christ. Perhaps his most imaginative drama is *Seed of Adam*, his first nativity play, and according to his own statement, it was not so much a presentation of the historic facts as of their spiritual value. One of Williams' most popular dramas is another nativity play, *The House by the Stable*. The power of the work lies in the intense struggle for man's soul and his allegiance to hell and to God. His last play, *The House of Octopus*, "is more typical of him than it is of the ordinary pious praise of missionary work."[14] Nominal Christians are unmasked and made to see themselves as they really are—and the unmasking is done through "The Flame"—Pentecostal fire. Besides novels and plays Charles Williams also wrote poetry, biography, criticism and philosophical and theological essays.

As intellectual in her approach to plays as Charles Williams, Dorothy Sayers began her work as a religious playwright with *The Zeal of Thy House*. The drama centers on William of Sens and the rebuilding of the Canterbury Cathedral in the twelfth century. Presented as a dedicated craftsman with loose morals, William has an affair with one of the cultivated ladies of Canterbury. During the building of the cathedral, William falls from a scaffold and is injured. One of the Canterbury priests believes that the fall is punishment for his loose moral life. William stays on as the dedicated craftsman, directing the workers from a pallet, for he seems incapable of believing the work can go on without his help. But Michael appears to him in a dream and explains that even God, as the incarnate Christ, left His work for others to finish. William then realizes he has committed "the eldest sin of all"—pride—and leaves the cathedral for others to finish.

Perhaps Dorothy Sayers' best-known dramatic work is *The Man Born to Be King,* a cycle of twelve radio plays on the life of Christ, written at the request of the British Broadcasting Company. Focusing attention on Christ's life in its historical setting, Dorothy Sayers' primary purpose appears to be to emphasize the humanity of Christ.

In addition to dramas Miss Sayers also wrote critical essays and mystery stories—and is probably better known as the creator of Lord Peter Wimsey than for her plays.

Some mention should be made of Christopher Fry. Although many of his critics contend that his dramas are so filled with gaiety that they can hardly be as serious as his disciples contend, Fry does often lead the reader into seeing large Christian truths. In *Thor, with Angels,* for example, Fry is concerned with man's gradual discovery of God. The play points up a contrast between the God of the Jutes and the Christian God and depicts Cymen, the leading character, discovering the Christian God in terms of forgiveness, mercy and compassion—all weaknesses in the religion of the Jutes. Some of Fry's comedies like *The Lady's Not for Burning* reveal significant aspects of the mystery in the relation between the infinite and the finite. Though Fry often laughs with man as he faces his paradoxes and incongruities, he nevertheless seriously affirms some of the central doctrines of the Christian faith—particularly the incarnation.

The twentieth century—at least in the 1960's—seems especially interested in myth and fantasy. One of the most popular works is the 1300-page epic-fantasy trilogy, *The Lord of the Rings,* written by a retired Oxford don, J. R. R. Tolkein. For several months the trilogy has been at the top of college best seller lists across the United States. Although Tolkein readers flock to *The Lord of the Rings* for a variety of reasons, many find in it a hopeful affirmation concerning man in his conflict with evil. The central image of the work is Christian: the principle of one person's taking evil upon himself and bearing it unto death for the salvation of the world.

There are creative artists of the twentieth century who unmistakably signalize that a segment of the literature of the century is God-oriented. In addition to creative artists there are critics such as Nathan Scott, Roland Frye, Martin Jarrett-Kerr and Amos Wilder who are vitally concerned with the problems of literature and belief. Even writers and critics who do not demonstrate a definite interest in the role of the Christian faith in literature acknowledge that there are reputable artists who *are* concerned. Stephen Spender, for example, in his book, *The Creative Element*, cogently states that in modern literature there is a reaction toward orthodoxy, and the most vital movement in literature in the West is religious. It is true, of course, that "religious" references do not necessarily constitute a God-oriented work of art. Exemplifying a consciousness of this fact, John Killinger advises that there is plenty of evidence in contemporary literature of Christianity's having been in the world for twenty centuries, for whether reading Joyce or Faulkner, Pasternak or Salinger, Ionesco or Eliot, one invariably encounters it. Killinger wisely cautions that evidence is of three kinds. He says:

> There are some works . . . in which it consists entirely of a few symbols or oblique references—mere scattered tracks that say Christ has walked this way. In others there is enough of Christ . . . to suggest something of the totality of his person and of his influence on human life, and to suggest it with some accuracy. And there are a few works of such blended artistry and devotion as probably to cause some readers to meet Christ in all his fullness there, and to kneel with Thomas and say, "my Lord and my God."[15]

While the modern reader bears these varieties of evidence in mind, he can still affirm that representative artists of the twentieth century are reasserting the role of faith in literature. These authors are writing God-oriented works.

Footnotes

Chapter One: THE MIDDLE AGES AND THE RENAISSANCE

[1]Harold C. Gardiner, Introduction to *The Confessions of St. Augustine*, E. B. Pusey (trans.) (New York: Washington Square Press, 1960), p. xiii.

[2]Frank N. Magill (ed.), *Masterpieces of Christian Literature* (New York: Harper & Row, 1963), p. 132.

[3]At this time it is my opinion that *Beowulf* should not be called religious literature in light of the definition of terms presented in the preface of this study. I am aware that a number of reputable scholars contend that the poem is written from a Christian perspective. Readers interested in pursuing further the possibilities of this interpretation may consult Dorothy Whitelock, *The Audience of Beowulf* (Oxford: Clarendon, 1951); also pertinent critical essays in Lewis E. Nicholson (ed.), *An Anthology of Beowulf Criticism* (Notre Dame, Ind.: University of Notre Dame, 1963).

[4]Vincent F. Hopper and Bernard D. N. Grebanier, *Essentials of European Literature* (New York: Barron's *Educational Series*, 1952), I, 62.

[5]John Ciardi, "How to Read Dante," *Saturday Review*, XLVIII (June 3, 1961), 13.

[6]Erich Auerbach, *Dante:Poet of the Secular World* (Chicago: University of Chicago, 1961), p. 110.

[7]*Ibid.*, p. 112.

[8]T. S. Eliot, "Dante" in *Selected Essays* (New York: Harcourt, Brace & World, 1932), p. 212.

[9]Hardin Craig, *English Drama of the Middle Ages* (London: Oxford University, 1955), p. 19.

[10]*Ibid.*, p. 20.

[11]Evelyn Underhill, *The Mystics of the Church* (New York: Schocken, 1964), p. 10.

[12]J. E. G. Montmorency, *Thomas à Kempis, His Age and Book* (London: Methuen & Co., 1906), p. 170.

[13]Hardin Craig, *The Literature of the English Renaissance, 1485-1660* (New York: Crowell-Collier, 1962), II, 32.

[14]*Ibid.*, pp. 35-36.

[15]*Ibid.*, p. 59.

[16]George Ian Duthie, *Shakespeare* (London: Hutchinson's University Library, 1951), pp. 162-63.

Chapter Two: THE SEVENTEENTH CENTURY

[1]Hardin Craig, *The Literature of the English Renaissance, 1485-1660* (New York: Crowell-Collier, 1962), II, 197.

[2]K. W. Gransden, *John Donne* (New York: Longmans, Green & Co., 1954), p. 173.

[3]Helen C. White *et al.*, *Seventeenth-Century Verse and Prose* (New York: Macmillan, 1951), I, 72.

[4]*Ibid.*

[5]Helen C. White, *The Metaphysical Poets* (New York: Collier, 1962), p. 118.

[6]Gransden, *op. cit.*, p. 126.

[7]White, *op. cit.*, p. 217.

[8]*Ibid.*, p. 271.

[9]*Ibid.*, p. 251.

[10]Basil Willey, *The Seventeenth Century Background* (Garden City, N. Y.: Doubleday & Co., 1953), p. 49.

[11]Frank N. Magill, *Masterpieces of Christian Literature* (New York: Harper & Row, 1963), p. 453.

[12]Margaret Bottrall, *Every Man a Phoenix* (London: John Murray, 1958), p. 113.

[13]T. R. Glover, *Poets and Puritans* (London: Methuen & Co., 1915), p. 117.

[14]Roger Sharrock, *John Bunyan* (London: Hutchinson University Library, 1954), p. 144.

[15]Roland M. Frye, *God, Man and Satan* (Princeton: Princeton University, 1960), pp. 130-31.

[16]G. B. Harrison, Introduction in *Pilgrim's Progress* (New York: Dutton & Co., 1962), p. x.

[17]Ola Winslow, *John Bunyan* (New York: Macmillan, 1961), p. 210.

[18]White *et al.*, *op. cit.*, p. 394.

[19]David Daiches, *Milton* (London: Hutchinson University Library, 1957), p. 203.

[20]Kenneth Muir, *John Milton* (New York: Longmans, Green & Co., 1955), p. 157. (Muir is quoting A. J. Waldock.)

[21]Daiches, *op. cit.*, p. 208.

[22]Daiches, *op. cit.*, p. 244.

[23]David E. Roberts, *Existentialism and Religious Belief* (New York: Oxford University, 1959), p. 43.

[24]*Ibid.*, p. 52.

[25]Evelyn Underhill, *The Mystics of the Church* (New York: Schocken, 1964), p. 210.

[26]Craig, *op. cit.*, p. 219.

Chapter Three: THE EIGHTEENTH CENTURY

[1]Walter Blair, Theodore Hornberger, Randall Stewart, *The Literature of the United States* (Chicago: Scott, Foresman & Co., 1946), I, 159.

[2]Perry Miller, *Jonathan Edwards* (New York: William Sloane Associates, 1949), pp. xii-xiii.

[3]Frank N. Magill, *Masterpieces of Christian Literature* (New York: Harper & Row, 1963), p. 615.

[4]This is the statement of John Meister and his colleagues who edited and abridged William Law's *A Serious Call to a Devout and Holy Life.* Their edition was published by Westminster Press in 1955. All quotations from Law's work included in this handbook are taken from Meister's edition.

[5]John Newton, "Preface to Poems" in *The Poetical Works of William Cowper*, William Benham (ed.) (New York: Macmillan, 1908), p. 48.

[6]Gilbert Thomas, *William Cowper and the Eighteenth Century* (London: George Allen & Unwin, 1948), pp. 262-63.

Chapter Four: THE NINETEENTH CENTURY

[1]Randall Stewart, *American Literature and Christian Doctrine* (Baton Rouge: Louisiana State University, 1958), p. 87.

[2]*Ibid.*, p. 88.

[3]*Ibid.*

[4]*Ibid.*
[5]Henry M. Battenhouse, *Poets of Christian Thought* (New York: Ronald, 1947), p. 123.
[6]*Ibid.*, p. 124.
[7]*Ibid.*, p. 128.
[8]*Ibid.*
[9]Marya Zaturenska, *Christina Rossetti* (New York: Macmillan, 1949), p. 236.
[10]G. K. Chesterton, Introduction to Greville MacDonald, *George MacDonald and His Wife* (London: George Allen & Unwin, 1924), pp. 14-15.
[11]Hoxie Neale Fairchild, *Religious Trends in English Poetry* (New York: Columbia University, 1957), p. 173.
[12]C. S. Lewis, *George MacDonald* (New York: Macmillan, 1960), p. 20.
[13]*Ibid.*, p. 14.
[14]*Ibid.*
[15]C. S. Lewis' collection of extracts from MacDonald's *Unspoken Sermons* is excellent. Footnote twelve gives bibliographical information.
[16]*Ibid.*, p. 18.
[17]Greville MacDonald, *George MacDonald and His Wife* (London: George Allen & Unwin, 1924), p. 299.
[18]*Ibid.*, p. 549.
[19]Lewis, *op. cit.*, p. 17.

Chapter Five: THE TWENTIETH CENTURY

[1]Edward McNall Burns, *Western Civilizations* (New York: Norton & Co., 1949), p. 818.
[2]*Ibid.*
[3]*Ibid.*, pp. 818-19.
[4]Henry Zylstra, *A Testament of Vision* (Grand Rapids: Eerdmans, 1958), p. 22.
[5]*Ibid.*
[6]*Ibid.*, p. 20.
[7]Randall Stewart, *American Literature and Christian Doctrine* (Baton Rouge: Louisiana State University, 1958), p. 130.
[8]Elizabeth Drew, *Poetry: A Modern Guide to Its Understanding and Enjoyment* (New York: Dell, 1959), p. 237.
[9]C. S. Kilby, *The Christian World of C. S. Lewis* (Grand Rapids: Eerdmans, 1964), p. 25.
[10]*Ibid.*
[11]Edmund Fuller, *Books with Men Behind Them* (New York: Random, 1962), p. 167.
[12]Monroe Spears, *The Poetry of W. H. Auden* (New York: Oxford University, 1963), p. 206.
[13]*Ibid.*, p. 205.
[14]Gerald Weales, *Religion in Modern English Drama* (Philadelphia: University of Pennsylvania, 1961), pp. 159-60.
[15]John Killinger, *The Failure of Theology in Modern Literature* (Nashville: Abingdon, 1963), p. 219.

For Further Reading

INSTEAD OF LISTING in addition to the footnotes a bibliography of the works used in preparation of this handbook, I should like to cite several sources pertinent to the general area of Religion and Literature or Belief and Literature. This will be followed by a selected bibliography of Readings in Background and Criticism relevant to the various chapters of this study. It is hoped that this selected bibliography will aid the reader in exploring more widely and penetrating more fully the works discussed or referred to in this work. By no means is the list intended to be exhaustive.

WORKS IN AREA OF RELIGION AND LITERATURE

Abrams, Meyer Howard (ed.). *Literature and Belief.* New York: Columbia University, 1958.

Gardiner, Harold C. *The Great Books, A Christian Appraisal.* New York: Devin-Adair, 1949-53. A symposium on the first fourth-year program of the Great Books Foundation.

Glicksberg, Charles. *Literature and Religion.* Dallas: Southern Methodist University, 1960.

Jarrett-Kerr, Martin. *Studies in Literature and Belief.* London: Rockliff, 1954.

MacIver, R. M. (ed.). *Great Moral Dilemmas in Literature, Past and Present.* New York: Institute for Religious & Social Studies. Distributed by Harper, 1956.

Maritain, Jacques. *The Responsibility of the Artist.* New York: Scribner, 1960.

Nicolson, Marjorie Hope. *Mountain Gloom and Mountain Glory.* Ithaca, N. Y.: Cornell University, 1959.

Sayers, Dorothy. *The Mind of the Maker.* New York: Harcourt, Brace & Co., 1941.

Scott, Nathan. *The Tragic Vision and the Christian Faith.* New York: Association Press, 1957.

——. *The New Orpheus, Essays Toward a Christian Poetic.* New York: Sheed & Ward, 1964.

Strong, Augustus Hopkins. *The Great Poets and Their Theology.* Philadelphia: Griffith & Rowland, 1897.

Wilder, Amos. *Modern Poetry and the Christian Tradition.* New York: Scribner, 1952.

THE MIDDLE AGES AND THE RENAISSANCE

Cochrane, Charles Norris. *Christianity and Classical Culture.* New York: Oxford University, 1944.

Lewis, C. S. *The Discarded Image, An Introduction to Medieval and Renaissance Literature.* Cambridge: Cambridge University, 1964.

Marrou, Henri. *St. Augustine and His Influence Through the Ages.* New York: Harper, 1957.

O'Meara, John J. *The Young Augustine: The Growth of St. Augustine's Mind up to His Conversion.* London: Longmans, 1954.

Sayers, Dorothy. *Introductory Papers on Dante.* New York: Harper, 1954.

——. *Further Papers on Dante.* New York: Harper, 1957.

Taylor, Henry Osborn. *The Mediaeval Mind.* New York: Macmillan, 1919.

Vossler, Karl. *Medieval Culture: An Introduction to Dante and His Time.* New York: Harcourt, Brace & Co., 1929.

THE SEVENTEENTH CENTURY

Alvarez, Alfred. *The School of Donne.* New York: Pantheon, 1961.

Bush, Douglas. *English Literature in the Earlier Seventeenth Century, 1600-1660.* New York: Oxford University, 1962.

Durr, R. A. *On the Mystical Poetry of Henry Vaughan.* Cambridge, Mass.: Harvard University, 1962.

Freeman, Rosemary. *English Emblem Books.* London: Chatto & Windus, 1948.

Gardner, Helen. *A Reading of Paradise Lost.* Oxford: Clarendon, 1965.

Grierson, Sir Herbert. *Cross-Currents in English Literature of the XVII Century.* London: Chatto & Windus, 1929.

Haller, William. *The Rise of Puritanism.* New York: Harper, 1957.

Hanford, James H. *A Milton Handbook.* New York: Appleton-Century-Crofts, 1946.

Hunt, Clay. *Donne's Poetry, Essays in Literary Analysis.* New Haven: Yale University, 1956.

Keast, William R. (ed.). *Seventeenth Century English Poetry.* New York: Oxford University, 1964.

Lewis, C. S. *A Preface to Paradise Lost.* New York: Oxford University, 1942.

Martz, Louis L. *The Poetry of Meditation.* New Haven: Yale University, 1954.

Summers, Joseph H. *George Herbert, His Religion and Art.* London: Chatto & Windus, 1954.

Tuve, Rosemond. *A Reading of George Herbert.* Chicago: University of Chicago, 1952.

Wallerstein, Ruth. *Richard Crashaw, A Study in Style and Poetic Development.* Madison, Wis.: University of Wisconsin, 1959.

Williamson, George C. *The Donne Tradition.* New York: Noonday Press, 1961.

———. *Seventeenth-Century Contexts.* London: Faber & Faber, 1960.

Westfall, Richard S. *Science and Religion in Seventeenth-Century England.* New Haven: Yale University, 1958.

THE EIGHTEENTH CENTURY

Boas, Ralph and Louise. *Cotton Mather, Keeper of the Puritan Conscience.* New York: Harper, 1928.

Cecil, David. *The Stricken Deer; or, the Life of Cowper.* London: Constable, 1929.

Cragg, Gerald Robertson. *Reason and Authority in the Eighteenth Century.* Cambridge: University Press, 1964.

Hazard, Paul. *European Thought in the Eighteenth Century.* New Haven: Yale University, 1954.

Nicolson, Sir Harold George. *The Age of Reason, 1700-1789.* London: Constable, 1960.

Parrington, Vernon L. *Main Currents in American Thought,* Vol. I. New York: Harcourt, Brace & Co., 1927.

Rudolph, Erwin. *A Study of the Religious Thought of William Law.* Urbana, Ill.: Unpublished Ph.D. dissertation. University of Illinois, 1962.

Townsend, Harvey (ed.). *The Philosophy of Jonathan Edwards from His Private Notebooks.* Eugene, Ore.: University of Oregon, 1955.

Willey, Basil. *Eighteenth Century Background.* New York: Columbia University, 1941.

THE NINETEENTH CENTURY

Brandes, George Morris Cohen. *Main Currents in Nineteenth-Century Literature.* New York: Macmillan, 1901-1905.

Brooks, Elleridge Streeter. *The Story of the Nineteenth Century of the Christian Era.* Boston: Lathrop, 1900.

Buck, Philo M. *The World's Great Age; the Story of a Century's Search for a Philosophy of Life.* New York: Macmillan, 1936.

Chesterton, Gilbert Keith. *Robert Browning.* New York: Macmillan, 1961.

Heuser, Alan. *The Shaping Vision of Gerard Manley Hopkins.* New York: Oxford University, 1958.

Moody, John. *John Henry Newman.* London: Sheed & Ward, 1946.

Somervell, David. *English Thought in the Nineteenth Century.* New York: Longmans-Green, 1936.

Stewart, Randall. *Nathaniel Hawthorne.* New Haven: Yale University, 1948.

Stuart, Dorothy Margaret. *Christina Rossetti.* London: Macmillan, 1930.

Whitla, William. *The Central Truth, The Incarnation in Robert Browning's Poetry.* Toronto: University of Toronto, 1963.

Willey, Basil. *The Nineteenth Century Studies.* New York: Columbia University, 1949.

THE TWENTIETH CENTURY

Andreach, Robert J. *Studies in Structure: The Stages in Spiritual Life in Four Modern Authors.* New York: Fordham University, 1964.

Blair, John G. *The Poetic Art of W. H. Auden.* Princeton: Princeton University, 1965.

Bloomfield, B. C. *W. H. Auden, A Bibliography, the Early Years Through 1955.* Charlottesville, Va.: University of Virginia, 1954.

Fuller, Edmund. *Man in Modern Fiction.* New York: Random, 1949.

Fullman, Christopher Edward. *The Mind and Art of Charles Williams: A Study of His Poetry, Plays and Novels.* Madison, Wis.: University of Wisconsin, 1954.

Gardner, Helen Louise. *The Art of T. S. Eliot.* London: Cresset, 1949.

Hopper, Stanley Romaine (ed.). *Spiritual Problems in Contemporary Literature.* New York: Harper, 1952.

Jarrett-Kerr, Martin. *François Mauriac.* New Haven: Yale University, 1954.

Sayers, Dorothy Leigh. *The Poetry of Search and the Poetry of Statement, and Other Posthumous Essays in Literature, Religion and Language.* London: Gollancz, 1963.

Scott, Nathan. *The Climate of Faith in Modern Literature.* New York: Seabury, 1964.

———. *Modern Literature and the Religious Frontier.* New York: Harper, 1958.

Williamson, George. *A Reader's Guide to T. S. Eliot: A Poem-by-Poem Analysis.* New York: Noonday, 1953.

Index

Ambrose, 9, 14
  Physiologus, 9
Andrewes, Lancelot, 89, 142
  Private Devotions, 89
  Seventeen Sermons on the Nativity, 89
Aristotle, 30
Auden, W. H., 169-74
  For the Time Being (The Christmas Oratorio), 170-74
Augustine, 9-16, 106
  Confessions, The, 9-16, 106
  Concerning the Beautiful and the Apt, 13
Aurelius, Marcus, 10
Lady Austen, 113

Balzac, Honoré de, 125
Baxter, Richard, 49-52
  Autobiography, 49
  Saints' Everlasting Rest, The, 49-52
Bay Psalm Book, 96
Bede, the Venerable, 17
  Ecclesiastical History, 17
Beowulf, 16, 177, n.
Bible, The, 14, 16, 30, 32, 41, 42, 55, 79, 83, 94, 102, 110, 170
  Authorized Version of 1611, 30
  Canticles, 102
  I Corinthians, 37
  Genesis, 16
  Gospels, 170
  Hebrews, 55, 149
  Job, 79
  King James Version, 94
  Luke, 79
  Matthew, 110
  Psalms, 41
  Romans, 14
  I Timothy, 102
Boethius, 16
  Consolation of Philosophy, The, 16

Brainerd, David, 122
  Diary of David Brainerd, The, 122
Browne, Sir Thomas, 46-49
  Religio Medici, 47-49
Browning, Robert, 134-37
  Christmas Eve, 137-38
  Cleon, 141
  A Death in the Desert, 139
  Easter Day, 138-39
  Epistle of Karshish, 141
  Parcelsus, 137
  Prospice, 141
  Rabbi Ben Ezra, 139-40
  Saul, 135-37
Bunyan, John, 52-61, 130, 131
  Grace Abounding, 53-55
  Heavenly Footman, The, 60
  Holy War, The, 60
  Life and Death of Mr. Badman, The, 60
  Pilgrim's Progress, The, 56-60, 130, 131
Burns, Robert, 124

Caedmon, 17
  Hymn to Caedmon, 17
Calvin, John, 29
Camus, Albert, 157
  Fall, The, 157
Chesterton, G. R., 150, 156
Ciardi, John, 20-21
Cicero, 12
  Hortensious, 12
Claudel, Paul, 156
Cloud of Unknowing, The, 26
Coleridge, Samuel Taylor, 46, 124
Cotton, John, 96
Cotton, Nathaniel, 113
Coverdale, Miles, 30
Cowper, William, 112-20
  Olney Hymns, 114
  Poems, 114-16
  Task, The, 116-20

Craig, Hardin, 24, 30, 94
Cranmer, Thomas, 30
   Book of Common Prayer, The,
   30
Crashaw, Richard, 44, 154
   Dear Bargain, 44
   The Weeper, 44
   Carmen Deo Nostro, 44
Cynewulf, 17
   Christ, The, 17

Daiches, David, 75, 77, 84, 85
Dante, Alighieri, 17-24
   Banquet, The, 18
   Divine Comedy, The, 18-24
   New Life, The, 18
   On Monarchy, 18
   On the Vulgar Tongue, 18
Darwin, Charles, 125
De Montmorency, J.E.G., 29
De Quincey, Thomas, 46
Dickens, Charles, 125
Dickinson, Emily, 154
Doddridge, Philip, 121
   *Rise and Progress of Religion in
   the Soul, The,* 121
Donne, John, 33-41, 41, 42, 113,
   142
   *Devotions upon Emergent Oc-
   casions,* 33-36
   Essays in Divinity, 36
   *Good Friday: 1613 Riding West-
   ward,* 40-41
   Holy Sonnets, 39
   Hymn to God the Father, 41-42
   *Hymn to God My God in My
   Sickness,* 41
   La Corona Sonnets, 40
   Sermons, 36-38
   Satyre III, 39
Dostoevsky, Fyodor, 154
   Brothers Karamazov, The, 154
Dreiser, Theodore, 156
   An American Tragedy, 156
Drew, Elizabeth, 162
Duthie, G. I., 31

Eckhardt, Johannes (Meister), 26
Edwards, Jonathan, 96, 99-105
   *Divine and Supernatural Light,
   A* (Sermon), 99
   Freedom of the Will, 101
   Personal Narrative, 101-4

*Sinners in the Hands of an An-
   gry God* (Sermon), 99
   *Treatise Concerning Religious
   Affection, A,* 100-101
   Two Dissertations, 104
Egerton, Sir Thomas, 33
Eliot, T. S., 24, 89, 156, 161-66,
   174, 176
   Ash Wednesday, 161-62
   Cocktail Party, The, 166
   For Lancelot Andrewes, 161
   Four Quartets, 161, 163-64, 174
   Hollow Men, The, 156, 161
   Journey of the Magi, 162-63
   Murder in the Cathedral, 164-66
   Waste Land, The, 156, 161
Epictetus, 9
Everyman, 25-26

Fairchild, Hoxie Neale, 151
Faulkner, William, 176
Fénelon, François, 93-94
   Maxims of the Saints, 93
Ferrar, Nicholas, 42
Fletcher, Giles, 79
   Christ's Victory and Triumph, 79
Flaubert, Gustave, 125
Fox, George, 92-93
   Journal, The, 92-93
Foxe, John, 30
   Book of Martyrs, 30
Fry, Christopher, 175
   Thor, with Angels, 175
   The Lady's Not for Burning, 175
Frye, Roland, 59, 176
Fuller, Edmund, 169

Gardiner, Harold C., 10
Gibbon, Edward, 108
Gifford, John, 52, 55
Glover, T. R., 55
Gordon, George (Lord Byron), 124
Gransden, K. W., 35
Gray, Thomas, 124
Goldsmith, Oliver, 124
Guyon, Madame, 93
   *Short and Easy Method of
   Prayer, A,* 93

Hall, Joseph, 89
   *Contemplations upon the Princi-
   pal Passages in the Holy
   Story,* 89

Meditations and Vows, 89
Hardy, Thomas, 125
Harrowing of Hell, The, 25
Hawthorne, Nathaniel, 129-34
  Celestial Railroad, The, 130-31, 132
  Earth's Holocaust, 133
  Ethan Brand, 129
  Rappaccini's Daughter, 129
  Scarlet Letter, The, 130, 133-34
Harrison, G. B., 60
Hazlitt, William, 46
Heine, Heinrich, 125
Hemingway, Ernest, 156
  Farewell to Arms, A, 156
Herbert, George, 42-44
  The Collar, 43
  Love, 43-44
  The Pulley, 43
  The Quip, 43
  The Temple, 42
  Virtue, 43
Herman, Nicholas (Brother Lawrence), 90-91
  Practice of the Presence of God, The, 90-91
Hervey, James, 122
  Meditations and Contemplations, 122
Heywood, John, 33
Hilton, Walter, 26
  Scale of Perfection, The, 26
Hopkins, Gerard Manley, 144-46
  God's Grandeur, 145
  Pied Beauty, 146
  The Windhover, 145-46
  The Wreck of the Deutschland, 144-45
Horace, 9
Howard, John, 116
Hugo, Victor, 125
Hutchinson, Anne, 98

Ionesco, Eugene, 176

Jarrett-Kerr, Martin 176
Jerome, 9
  Latin Vulgate, 9
Johnson, Samuel, 46, 108, 121
  Dictionary, 121
  Lives of the Most Eminent Poets, The, 121
Johnson, Thomas, 87

Jonson, Ben, 30
Jowett, Benjamin, 144
Joyce, James, 156, 176
  Ulysses, 156
Juliana of Norwich, 26
Juvenal, 9

Keats, John, 124
Keble, John, 127, 150
  Christian Year, The, 150
Kempis, Thomas à, 26-29, 121
  Imitation of Christ, The, 27-29
Killinger, John, 176
Kingsley, Charles, 126

Lamb, Charles, 46, 105
  Essays of Elia, 105
Latimer, Hugh, 30
Law, William, 107-12, 121, 127
  Christian Perfection, 108
  Serious Call to a Devout and Holy Life, A, 108-12, 129
Lewis, C. S., 46, 151, 166-67
  Allegory of Love, The, 167
  Pilgrim's Regress, The, 167
  Screwtape Letters, The, 167-69
  Surprised by Joy, 166
  Volume on Sixteenth Century in *Oxford History of English Literature,* 167
Livy, 9
Lowell, James Russell, 46
Luther, Martin, 29
Lycurgus, 98

MacDonald, George, 150-52
  Diary of an Old Soul, The, 151-52
  Lilith, 152
  Phantastes, 152
  Unspoken Sermons, 152
Malraux, André, 156
  Man's Hope, 156
Mann, Thomas, 156
  Magic Mountain, 156
Marini, 44
Martial, 9
Mather, Cotton, 96-99, 100, 105
  Christian Philosopher, The, 99
  Essay To Do Good, 99
  Magnall Christi Americana, 97-99

Mather, Increase, 96, 100
Mauriac, François, 156, 157-61
    Viper's Tangle, 158, 160
    Woman of the Pharisees, 158, 159-60
Meister, John, 178, n.
Melville, Herman, 46
Meredith, George, 125
Miller, Perry, 104
Milton, John, 63-87
    Academic Prolusions, 64
    Areopagitica, 65-66
    Comus, 64, 75
    History of Britain, 66
    Il Penseroso, 64
    L'allegro, 64
    Lycidas, 64
    Ode on the Morning of Christ's Nativity, 66-67
    Of Christian Doctrine, 66
    Of Education, 65-66
    On His Being Arrived at the Age of Twenty-Three, 64
    Paradise Lost, 66, 67-78
    Paradise Regained, 66, 79-83
    Samson Agonistes, 66, 83-87
    Sonnet XIX: When I Consider . . . , 67

Newman, John Henry, 125-29, 144
    Apologia Pro Vita Sua, 126-29
    Tracts for the Times, 126, 127
Newton, John, 113, 114
Nicholson, Lewis E., 177, n.

Origen, 9
    De Principiis, 9
Ovid, 9

Pascal, Blaise, 91-92
    Pensées, 91-92
Pasternak, Boris, 176
Pater, Walter, 46, 144
Phips, Sir William, 98
Plato, 30
Poe, Edgar Allan, 46
Powell, Mary, 66
Pusey, Edward, 127

Quarles, Francis, 89
Quem Quaeritis, 24

Reynolds, John, 94

Ridley, Nicholas, 30
Rolle, Richard, 26
Romance of the Rose, The, 17
Rossetti, Christina, 141-44
    Better Resurrection, A, 143
    Christ Our All in All, 142-43
    Christmas Carol, A, 143-44
    Face of the Deep, The, 142
    Times Flies: A Reading Diary, 142
    Goblin Market, 142
    Heart Knoweth Its Own Bitterness, The, 144
    Lord, Save Us, We Perish, 142
    Not Yours but You, 143-44
    Sleep at Sea, 144
    There Remaineth Therefore a Rest for the People of God, 144
    Uphill, 144
Rousseau, Jean Jacques, 124
Rutherford, Samuel, 90
    Letters, 90
Ruysbroeck, 26

Salinger, J. D., 176
Sand, George, 125
Sayers, Dorothy, 174-75
    The Zeal of Thy House, 174-75
    The Man Born To Be King, 175
Schiller, Friedrich, 124
Scott, Nathan, 176
Second Shepherd's Play, 25
Seneca, 9
Shakespeare, William, 31
    Macbeth, 31
Shelley, Percy Bysshe, 124
Sidney, Sir Philip, 118
Sienkiewicz, Henryk, 146-50
    Quo Vadis, 146-50
Smith, Hannah Whitall, 152-53
    Christian's Secret of a Happy Life, The, 152-53
Spender, Stephen, 176
Spenser, Edmund, 30
    Faerie Queene, The, 30, 79
Steinbeck, John, 156
    Grapes of Wrath, 156
Stewart, Randall, 134, 161
Southwell, Robert, 30
    Burning Babe, The, 30
    St. Peter's Complaint, 30
Suso, Heinrich, 26

Tacitus, 9
Tauler, Johann, 26
Taylor, Edward, 87-88
  God's Determination, 87
  Huswifery, 88
  Poetical Works, The, 87-88
  Sacramental Meditations, 88
Taylor, Henry Wyllys, 87
Taylor, Jeremy, 61-63, 121
  Liberty of Prophesying, 61
  Rule and Exercise of Holy Living and Holy Dying, The, 62-64
Thackeray, William, 125
Thompson, Francis, 153-54
  Hound of Heaven, The, 153-54
Thornton, John, 116
Tolkein, J.R.R., 175-76
  Lord of the Rings, The, 175-76
Traherne, Thomas, 45-46
  Right Apprehension, 46
  Wonder, The, 46
Tyndale, William, 29

Underhill, Evelyn, 26
Unwin, Morley, 113

Vaughan, Henry, 44-45
  Anguish, 45
  Cock-Crowing, 45
  Corruption, 45
  Love and Discipline, 45
Virgil, 9

Waugh, Evelyn, 156
Wesley, John, 108, 113, 121, 122
  Journal, 121
  Christian Perfection, 121
White, Helen, 39
Whitefield, George, 108, 113
Whitelock, Dorothy, 177, n.
Wigglesworth, Michael, 96
  Day of Doom, 96
Wilder, Amos, 176
Willey, Basil, 47
Williams, Charles, 174
  House by the Stable, The, 174
  House of Octopus, The, 174
  Rite of the Passion, 174
  War in Heaven, 174
Williams, Roger, 98
Winslow, Ola, 61
Winthrop, John, 98
Wolfe, Thomas, 156-67
  Of Time and the River, 156-57
  You Can't Go Home Again, 156-57
Woodcock, Katherine, 66
Woolman, John, 96, 105-7
  Journal, 105-7
Wordsworth, William, 44, 124

Zola, Emile, 125
Zwingli, Ulrich, 29
Zylstra, Henry, 157